Ready, Relevant and Resurgent

A Blueprint for the Transformation of India's Military

READY, RELEVANT AND RESURGENT

A BLUEPRINT FOR THE TRANSFORMATION OF INDIA'S MILITARY

General Anil Chauhan

Chief of Defence Staff

Foreword by

Rajnath Singh

Raksha Mantri, India

CENTRE FOR JOINT WARFARE STUDIES

PENTAGON PRESS LLP

First Print May 2025
Second Reprint June 2025
Third Reprint July 2025
Fourth Reprint November 2025
Fifth Reprint April 2026

PENTAGON PRESS LLP
206, Peacock Lane, Shahpur Jat
New Delhi-110049, India
Contact: 011-26490600

Typeset in Adobe Garamond, 12 Point
Printed at Aegean Offset Printers, Greater Noida

ISBN 978-81-984458-6-5

Disclaimer: *The views expressed in the book are personal views of the author and in no way reflects the opinion of the Ministry of Defence or of the Government of India as the author is the serving CDS at present.*

www.pentagonpress.in

Contents

SECTION D: IMPORTANT TALKS

Foreword

Jointness, integration and theaterisation are the building blocks for the modernisation and transformation of the Indian armed forces. The vision of a Viksit Bharat by 2047 will be shaped by a Sashakt and Atmanirbhar Bharat. The capacity and capabilities of the Indian military, fighting with indigenous platforms and technologies, undergirded by indigenous knowledge systems and powered by robust and resilient supply chains will define India's continuous and responsible ascent on the world stage.

The current book, a collection of writings by General Anil Chauhan, India's Chief of Defence Staff (CDS) deals with several subjects that put together, can propel the armed forces to be future-ready – organisationally, conceptually and culturally thus acquiring the capability to dominate traditional and emerging domains of warfare against current and future adversaries. This calls for all of us to not only challenge the status quo but to be open-minded to reforms. The quest for excellence must prevail in all ranks of the armed forces. The reforms being attempted by the armed forces are nothing short of a revolution and the current work will not only act as a source of information on the range of reforms but also as a catalyst to speed up the process.

The pace of technological change has far outstripped the ability of political systems to manage, regulate and harness them. The same seems to hold for militaries worldwide. The ongoing conflicts have shown that the militaries that can innovate and adapt systems and technologies on the battlefield will gain and retain an edge over their adversary. It is worthwhile to mention that technology will need to be innovated upon and harnessed by talented individuals and that is why the need for inducting a more technologically savvy manpower within the armed forces is a priority for us. The Agnipath scheme lays down the path for such individuals to join the forces. I am confident that this scheme will ensure that the best and brightest Indian citizens will join the forces and enrich both the forces and themselves in the process.

The Chief of Defence Staff has presented a vision that is both inspiring and actionable, one that will undoubtedly shape the future of India's defence strategy. I commend this work to all those who are dedicated to the cause of national security and defence. I am sanguine that it will be a vital resource for policymakers, military leaders and scholars alike, offering insights that are both profound and practical.

Rajnath Singh
Raksha Mantri, India

Introduction

Addressing the senior hierarchy of India's three armed services in New Delhi in 2014 during his first Combined Commanders' Conference, Prime Minister Narendra Modi presented his vision for India's security imperatives in the coming years. One of the most critical components of the Hon'ble PM's vision was the transformation of the three services into a modern force capable of pursuing India's national interests across multiple domains including traditional and emerging ones. The process of transformation was to be premised on laying a strong foundation of jointness and integration at all levels among the three services. The aim was to prepare the Indian armed forces for meeting future threats and challenges. Turning words into deeds, six years down the line, the government created the Department of Military Affairs (DMA) and the post of the Chief of Defence Staff (CDS). The objective of this reform in the higher defence management was to bring about jointness among the armed forces and to foster expertise in military affairs.

During the Combined Commanders' Conference in the closing days of March 2023, also my first conference as the CDS, the theme chosen was "Ready, Relevant, Resurgent". Penning down the various chapters of this book, I have realised that these three terms signify the future of our forces. The Armed Forces have always been the first responders facing challenges to the sovereignty and territorial integrity of the nation and have demonstrably acquitted themselves with aplomb. However, as we navigate the stormy geo-political arena of the 21st century, there is a rising uncertainty in the nature, type and timing of future threats. To put this in context, one must turn to the notion of security which has diffused and proliferated across domains and fields. The notion of conventional security has expanded to food, water, human, and climate security, while the domains or arenas where armed forces fight each other have also multiplied to include cyber, electromagnetic spectrum, near space, and outer space, apart from the traditional ones of land, air and sea. This requires a quantum jump in our intellectual, organisational and material capabilities. Operations other than war such as aiding and assisting civil authorities during disasters and countering grey zone operations require that we mould and transform ourselves to stay relevant in the pursuit of national interests. Finally, the last issue is of resurgence. Like the proverbial phoenix, we need to shed certain vestiges and predilections, go back to the basics and see what our ancestors knew, wrote and spoke about warfare, statecraft and diplomacy. Resurgence will lead to resilience, which is what we aspire for.

It has been 22 months since I was appointed as the CDS. One of the tasks entrusted to the CDS has been to facilitate the restructuring of military commands for the optimal utilisation of resources and bring about jointness and integration in operations. This will be visibly manifested in the establishment of joint operational structures at various levels and echelons. This switch will be one of the most revolutionary changes attempted by the Indian armed forces in the post-independence era. The creation of the Theater Commands is the beginning of this change and will kick-start next generation of reforms in the armed forces.

The concept of establishing theatre commands is to create two parallel and complementary streams for 'Force Application' and 'Force Generation'. The Force Application component will become the responsibility of a theatre commander, whereas Service Chiefs, in their transformed role will be responsible for what is colloquially called the 'Raise, Train and Sustain (RTS) function'. In other words, the service chiefs will preside over the Force Generation, an equally important aspect.

An essential prerequisite for the establishment of theatre commands is a high degree of jointness amongst the three Services and physical integration of several processes, activities and essential infrastructure. The structural transformation at the apex level will usher in conceptual, doctrinal and cultural changes. It will also trigger cascading organisational changes at HQs/establishments at lower levels. The transformation that will be triggered in the operational and administrative functioning will come with its own set of challenges. The acceptability of the change will only happen once officers at all levels are aware of the impending changes. The maximum impact of these changes will be on middle-level officers who not only will need to adopt and adapt to a new normal but also take the lead in a transformed environment. I believe that there is a need to take everyone along, especially the middle-level officers so that they become a catalyst for change rather than being sceptical and resisting it. Articles such as 'Jointness and Integration 2.0', 'HDO: Past, Present and Future and ' Transformation and Management of Change' form part of my endeavour to take everyone along by keeping them informed.

The reforms in the Armed Forces need to be seen from a wider perspective. Today, war and warfare are continuously evolving at an increasingly rapid pace. As a result, the armed forces need to absorb new and emerging technologies, as well as, evolve new tactics to be future-ready. The future of warfare itself needs deliberation, diligent prognosis and an informed assimilation. The armed forces need to build capabilities to conduct integrated Multi-Domain Operations across the spectrum of conflict. Our organisational structures, capabilities and strategies must be dovetailed into our understanding of the future. Articles such as 'Preparing for the Third Revolution in Military Affairs', 'Evolving Battlefield Architecture', 'The Nature of War and Types of Conflicts' and 'Tactics Led Force Modernisation' are an expression of my thoughts on what lies ahead in the domain of warfare.

India aspires to be a developed nation (Viksit Bharat) by 2047. The foundation of an economically vibrant and politically stable Bharat must rest on a strong military. The four instruments of National Power that are Diplomatic, International, Military and Economic must work in unison towards a common vision for Bharat to realise its desired destiny. A self-reliant, self-assured, self-confident Indian military will be supported by the principle of 'Atmanirbharta'. The relevance of self-reliance in India's growth is the subject of deliberation in articles such as 'Atmanirbharta in Defence', and 'Indigenisation and Innovation: The Road Ahead'.

The conceptual and intellectual moorings of India's military need the anchorage of Indian ideas and thoughts. The geo-political environment which we face and the challenges and opportunities that lay before us are unique to us. We need to find Indian solutions to Indian problems. Our ancient wisdom is a source of motivation and inspiration. Our position in the comity of nations and thus our stakes in international affairs stem from our heritage. It reflects our deep-rooted strategic and cultural characteristics. These thoughts have been emphasised in an article on 'Ancient Indian Wisdom and its Relevance in Modern Strategy and Statecraft.

The concepts ideated in the book aim to focus on the long-term efficacy of military reforms to foster jointness and interoperability, facilitate optimisation and ensure credible modernisation of the armed forces to meet emerging challenges and contribute to the security of the nation. I am confident that the readers will find these ideas stimulating which in turn will result in further deliberations. This book is just the beginning of such nuanced thoughts.

General Anil Chauhan
Chief of Defence Staff

List of Abbreviations

4Is	Innovative, Inventive, Imaginative and Indigenous
5Cs	Competition, Crisis, Confrontation, Conflict and Combat
AD	Air Defence
ADB	Army Design Bureau
ADC	Aide-de-Camp
ADITI	Acing Development of Innovating Technologies
AESA	Active Electronically Steered Array
ALH	Advanced Light Helicopter
AoB	Allocation of Business
ARTRAC	Army Training Command
ASEAN	Association of South East Asian Nations
ATAGS	Advanced Towed Artillery Gun System
BDA	Battle Damage Assessment
BEML	Bharat Earth Movers Limited
BFT	Battle Field Transparency
BIMSTEC	Bay of Bengal Initiative for Multi-Sectoral Technical and Economic Cooperation
BRD	Base Repair Depot
BRICS	Brazil, Russia, India, China and South Africa
BSS	Battlefield Surveillance System
C4I	Command, Control, Communication, Computers and Intelligence
C4ISR	Command, Control, Communication, Computers, Intelligence, Surveillance and Reconnaissance
CAATSA	Countering America's Adversaries Through Sanctions Act

CBRN	Chemical, Biological, Radiological and Nuclear
CCPA	Cabinet Committee on Political Affairs
CCS	Cabinet Committee on Security
CDM	College of Defence Management
CDS	Chief of Defence Staff
CENTO	Central Treaty Organisation
CET	Critical and Emerging Technologies
C-in-C	Commander-in-Chief
CISC	Corps Intelligence and Surveillance Centre
CISC	Chief of IDS to Chairman COSC
CNP	Comprehensive National Power
COAP	Composite Offensive Air Package
COSC	Chiefs of Staff Committee
CsOE	Centers of Excellence
CTBT	Comprehensive Test Ban Treaty
DAIC	Defence AI Council
DAP	Defence Acquisition Procedure
DCB	Ditch-cum-Bund
DCC	Defence Committee of the Cabinet
DCPP	Development cum Production Partner
DCW	Data Centric Warfare
DIC	Defence Industrial Corridor
DISC	Division Intelligence and Surveillance Centre
DMA	Department of Military Affairs
DMC	Defence Minister Committee
DPC	Defence Planning Committee
DPEPP	Defence Production and Export Promotion Policy
DPM	Defence Procurement Manual
DPS	Defence Planning Staff
DPSU	Defence Public Sectors Undertaking
DRDO	Defence Research and Development Organisation
DSSC	Defence Services Staff College

DTIS	Defence Testing Infrastructure Scheme
EAM	External Affairs Minister
EAS	East Asia Summit
EDT	Emerging & Disruptive Technologies
EEZ	Exclusive Economic Zone
EM	Electromagnetic
EW	Electronic Warfare
FDI	Foreign Direct Investment
FDN	Floating Dock for the Navy
FOBS	Fractional Orbit Bombardment Systems
FSO	Front Section Optronics
GCAP	Global Combat Air Programme
GE	General Electric
GERD	Gross Expenditure on R & D
GIS	Geographic Information System
GoM	Group of Ministers
GPAI	Global Partnership on Artificial intelligence
GPS	Global Positioning System
GSQR	General Staff Qualitative Requirements
GWOT	Global War on Terror
HADR	Humanitarian Assistance and Disaster Relief
HAL	Hindustan Aeronautics Limited
HALE	High Altitude Long Endurance
HDO	Higher Defence Organisation
HGV	Hypersonic Glide Vehicle
I2U2	India, Israel, US, UAE
IACCS	Integrated Air Command and Control System
ICT	Information and Communication Technology
ICV	Infantry Combat Vehicle
IDDM	Indigenous Designed, Developed and Manufactured
iDEX	Innovations for Defence Excellence
IDS	Integrated Defence Staff

IFC	International Fusion Centre
IFF	Identification of Friend and Foe
IGC	Indira Gandhi Canal
IMEC	India Middle East Europe Economic Corridor
IMSAS	Indian Maritime Situational Awareness System
INSTC	International North-South Transport Corridor
IONS	Indian Ocean Naval Symposium
IOR	Indian Ocean Region
IORA	Indian Ocean Rim Association
IoT	Internet of Things
IPOI	Indo Pacific Oceans Initiative
ITC	Integrated Theatre Command
JOCAP	Joint Capsule
JOCOM	Joint Operations Committee
JV	Joint Venture
LAC	Line of Actual Control
LC	Line of Control
LCA	Light Combat Aircraft
LCH	Light Combat Helicopter
LIDAR	Light Detection and Ranging
MALE	Medium Altitude Long Endurance
MANPADS	Man Portable Air Defence System
MBRL	Multi Barrel Rocket Launcher
MDA	Maritime Domain Awareness
MDO	Multi Domain Operations
MGO	Master General Ordnance
MIC	Military Industrial Complex
MLU	Mid Life Upgrade
MoD	Ministry of Defence
MRL	Manufacturing Readiness Level
MRSAM	Medium Range Surface to Air Missiles
MSME	Micro, Small and Medium Enterprises

MUM-T	Manned-Unmanned Teaming
NATO	North Atlantic Treaty Organisation
NCW	Network Centric Warfare
NCW	Net Centric Warfare
NDS	National Defence Strategy
NITI	National Institute for Transforming India
NMS	National Military Strategy
NSA	National Security Advisor
NSAI	National Strategy for Artificial Intelligence
NSC	National Security Council
NSCS	National Security Council Secretariat
NSS	National Security Strategy
OEM	Original Equipment Manufacturer
OFB	Ordnance Factory Board
ONA	Office of Net Assessment
OODA	Observe, Orient, Decide and Act
PGM	Precision Guided Munition
PIF	Pacific Island Forum
PIL	Positive Indigenisation List
PLA	People's Liberation Army
PLAAF	People's Liberation Army Air Force
PME	Professional Military Education
PMF	Para Military Forces
PPP	Public Private Partnership
PSU	Public Sector Undertaking
QR	Qualitative Requirement
QUAD	Quadrilateral Security Dialogue
R&D	Research and Development
RAPID	Re-organised Army plains Infantry Division
RMA	Revolution in Military Affairs
S&T	Science and Technology
SAGAR	Security and Growth for All in the Region

SAR	Synthetic Aperture Radar
SCAF	Systeme-de-Combat-Aerien-du-Futur (French)
SCO	Shanghai Cooperation Organisation
SDI	Software Development Institute
SDR	Software Defined Radio
SEATO	Southeast Asia Treaty Organisation
SFC	Strategic Forces Command
SHQ	Service Headquarter
SLOC	Sea Lanes of Communication
SME	Subject Matter Expert
TASL	Tata Advanced Systems Ltd
TDF	Technology Development Fund
ToB	Transaction of Business
ToT	Transfer of Technology
TRL	Technology Readiness Level
TTP	Tactics, Techniques and Procedures
TTP	Thousand Talent Plan
UAV	Unmanned Aerial Vehicle
UNGA	United Nation General Assembly
USI	United Service Institution of India
USV	Unmanned Surface Vessel
VCDS	Vice Chief of Defence Staff
VSHORAD	Very Short Range Air Defence System
VUCA	Volatile, Uncertain, Complex and Ambiguous
WESEE	Weapons and Electronic Systems Engineering Establishment

Section A

GENERAL

1

Military Geography

"The conduct of warfare is dependent on the physical and cultural characteristics of the conflict area which constitutes the military operating environment."

—By the author

Introduction

Geography, literally the study of lands, features, inhabitants and phenomena of Earth, as a subject can broadly be divided in several ways but the most predominant division includes Physical Geography and Human Geography. Physical geography is a study of natural features like rivers, mountains, landforms and the environment surrounding it, which includes climate and weather, though not limited to these. Human geography deals with spatial distribution of population and dwells into aspects like religion, language, culture, ethnicity, political system, economy etc. The space-location-attribute aspects of physical geography impacts the strategic importance of a place which in turn affects the politics surrounding it, whereas the people-demography-ideology aspect of human geography affects intra and inter-state relations. Hence in very broad terms, geography bridges the gap between arts and sciences, connecting the study of history and culture with environmental factors. Physical and Human Geography are equally important subjects for Military Commanders as military operations by their very nature are geographic - they transpire in 'space', consisting of a unique physical and human landscape.

Military Geography

The study of military geography evolved in the early 19th Century and the initial focus was on description of terrain, regional studies and case studies to demonstrate the effects of the physical landscape on battles. During this period the literature on physical geography was typically devoid of critical analyses and the aspect of human geography was not given the due importance it deserved. This trend continued through the First World War. However, the Second World War was a defining moment for military geography, due to the trans-continental and global scale of the conflict and war effort. Thus military geography gained prominence and became a more analytical and intrinsic part of strategic and operational planning.

The conduct of warfare is dependent on the physical and cultural characteristics of the conflict area which constitutes the military operating environment. Military organisations, their operational doctrines, force structures, requirements of weapons and equipment are dependent on the physical and cultural conditions in which they are likely to operate, whereas military operations are a three dimensional array of actions that have to be arranged in time and space. Geographers understand the component and processes – terrain, weather, climate and people that affect military operations in time and space. Military geography thus is an application of geographic information, tools and technologies to military problems across the spectrum of military operations from peacetime to wartime. Military Geography combines select aspects of physical and human geographies to study its impact on conduct of military operations. It is thus a broad and dynamic subject which is inter-related to areas such as military technology, military history, geology, cultural, political geography and geopolitics. The value of military geography lies in understanding the spatial perspective of the military operating environment and drawing relevant deductions impacting the conduct of operations. The mere listing of information and data concerning a theatre of operations does not in itself constitute a study of military geography. Hence, military geography can be construed as the study of the ways in which a strategic design and military plans are enmeshed with geographical entities to derive maximum advantage. In conflict, military geography provides the foundation for, and the means to develop a coherent and selective mission-oriented assessment of the environmental matrix at the tactical, operational and strategic levels.

The terrain in the theatre of operations is generally neutral as it affords equal advantage to the adversaries. To exploit the terrain to own advantage, it is imperative to study all aspects of the terrain in the intended theatre of operations to arrive at advantages and disadvantages it presents to both sides. Their comparative analysis in military parlance is called 'Terrain Analysis'. It is both a Science as well as an Art as some deductions are an outcome of logical conclusions whereas some are arrived at through experience of operating in diverse terrains and operational situations. It is this eye for detail that separates a successful military commander from the rest.

While planning a military operation, the study of the terrain is the foremost ingredient of the mission analysis. General trafficability of the terrain, layout of communication arteries including important communication centers, population distribution, important urban centers, towns and villages, centers of economic activity, availability of natural resources, climate etc help to draw out relevant deductions for formulating an appropriate operational strategy. The deductions could include ground of vital importance, features that provide depth to it, objectives, routes leading to it, axis of operations and maintenance, timings, etc. These innate factors when considered with the adversary's likely intent, availability of forces and their deployment helps formulation of what in army parlance is called 'Military Appreciation'. This appreciation helps to draw out relevant deductions like own and enemy's operational centres of gravity, operational phases and finally synchronization and coordination of combat, combat support and logistics echelons in support of the military plan.

At the tactical level, defensibility of an area including deployability, advantages of elevation, ease of navigation, camouflage and concealment, approaches to an objective or defended locality, intervisibility are some of the factors that help evaluate ground. It leads to deductions on areas that need to be occupied and held, areas that need to be captured, areas that need to be denied by fire or areas that need to be kept under surveillance. 'Time and space' and 'troops to task' get added on before executing the mission. Even at the sub-tactical level, it is ingrained to analyse objective, route and fire plan before executing a mission.

The application of military geography is not restricted to war time only. Humanitarian Assistance and Disaster Relief (HADR) operations to include aid to civil authorities like flood relief, narcotics control, peace keeping, counter terror operations, evacuation and relocation of non-combatant population, control of refugees, illegal immigration etc. are some missions that require intimate knowledge of physical and human geography.

There is an underappreciated aspect of geography in military operations, which relates possession of natural resources to strategic advantage. There have been numerous examples in contemporary history where natural resources have become a bone of contention and a vaunted prize by many nations. From the Scramble for Africa in the late 19th and early 20th centuries, to Germany attacking fellow ally USSR in 1941 over *lebensraum* (extra living space) and the Japanese attack on the US naval base in Pearl Harbour over the latter's sanctioning of raw materials for the former's economic and military growth, the desire for natural resources has initiated and fueled conflicts. The Civil War fought between the northern and southern 'states' in the US in the mid-18th century was over the issue of slave labour and the right of Southern States (or the Confederacy) to keep treating humans as property. This case highlights the connect between human and terrestrial geography. Today, the requirement of rare earth metals, minerals and materials for technological innovation has again brought geography to the forefront of strategic competition and conflict.

Geographical Changes and Military Operations

The subject of military geography remains relevant to a great extent amongst military practitioners. It however has witnessed a general decline among bureaucracy, strategic community and the academicians. In some intellectual circles there is also a general disdain to consider Geography as a decisive factor in influencing the course of human history. It suggests that nature is more powerful than man and hence mankind has a limit in deciding their own fate. There could be two reasons for the declining interest in the subject of Military Geography; one is the character of conventional wars, which earlier required application of military forces that maneuvered over vast distances to achieve its politico-military objectives like the German invasion of Russia, North African campaign and the Japanese consolidation of its so called Greater Asia co-prosperity sphere. It can be argued that the new age warfare in all its dimensions ranging from use of long range missiles, air power and nuclear weapons at one end of the spectrum to terrorism at the other end does not require an in depth knowledge of geography. This thought questions the basic premise of the utility of geography in the formulation of a military strategy. The second reason could stem from a belief that physical geography is difficult and time consuming to alter. Since the advantages and vulnerabilities accruing out of geography will be finite and have already been discovered, there is nothing esoteric in perusing the subject. Both these suppositions are misplaced.

Geography had remained as a 'constant' for a very long time on our planet. However, the advent of industrial age and advances in science and technology, have ushered in major changes in the physical geography and landforms across the Globe. The Suez Canal connected the Mediterranean Sea to Indian Ocean in 1869 and the Panama Canal linked the Pacific and the Atlantic. Britain, an island nation for centuries is today, technically not so. Most alterations in physical geography aim to reduce the distance-time continuum with a view to economise on the movement of goods and people between places. Canals connecting oceans, tunnels that connect regions separated by natural barriers of mountains and seas, high speed transportation corridors based on rail and roads, waterways and air transportation hubs have, while altering the geography, also altered the geo-strategic significance of these places. Accelerated changes in the physical geography have had a considerable impact on human geography. The combined changes in both these have had a major impact on the geo-politics of the region with enhanced bearing on the aspects related to geo-strategy and military operations.

A prime example of how challenges imposed by geography can be overcome is best seen in Tibet. Till 1950, Tibet was isolated and relatively secure as China had little access to it. However, with its occupation in 1950, China brought itself to India's doorstep. Having realized the importance of this frontier region along India's borders, China has undertaken sustained developmental activities to improve surface communications and air services. China has overcome the impediments of long distances, harsh climate, rarified atmosphere, inhospitable terrain and geological problems of permafrost to connect Tibet by road, rail and air to the mainland on its East. The rate of infrastructure development and resultant transformation of Tibet has witnessed a major acceleration in the last three decades. There was a belief that the Himalayas are impregnable, but that too seems to be on the verge of being altered by China by constructing roads right up to the passes along Indo-Tibetan border. This has eroded the concept of impregnability of the Himalayas. The strategic thought process till the last decade of the previous century was based on the hypothesis that the threat from China will develop over two seasons. This is no longer relevant. The improved infrastructure in Tibet in terms of improved surface communication and airfields as also forward deployment of troops and relocation of warwaging formations, gives India less reaction time. Apart from physical infrastructure, we also witness modern clustered settlements, the so called Xiaokang villages, that have sprung in the vicinity of the frontiers along with related supporting infrastructure to settle nomadic population thus interfering in the human geography of Tibet as well. The Tibetan inhabitants of these 'Model Villages' can be confined physically as well as ideologically by modern surveillance systems and by regulating information flow. The Belt and Road Initiative, a flagship project of President Xi Jinping, also looks at exploiting geography for greater benefits for the Chinese markets, economy and polity, in the guise of infrastructure development across the World.

Our Western border with Pakistan has also witnessed major geographical changes impacting conventional operations. The alluvial plains of Punjab sandwiched between the mountain ranges of Shivalik,

Pir Panjal and Himalayas and the deserts of Cholistan and Thar were a favourite invasion route in the past. Even after independence, the terrain in Punjab being open was ideal for large scale manoeuver by mechanised formations. This was exploited by the Indian Army during the 1965 India - Pakistan War. The Ichhogil Canal is synonymous with the 1965 war. This canal which ran about 8 kilometres inside Pakistan was a formidable defensive structure and brought out the potency of artificial obstacles in open terrain. This led Pakistan to use the Ichhogil model to construct number of such obstacles in the form of Ditch-cum-Bunds (DCBs) and canals for irrigation as well as to increase the terrain friction and thus prevent unhindered advance of the Indian mechanised formations. India followed suit and the terrain in the border areas on both sides is now gridlocked with canals, ditches and DCBs making maneuvers by mechanised formations difficult.

Similar changes in geography are being advanced in Rajasthan where the Indira Gandhi Canal (IGC) traverses through seven districts. The canal not only provides irrigation to water parched areas in the states, but its alignment has a strategic and geo political orientation. On the Pakistan side, the Eastern Sadiqia which further bifurcates into Sirajwah distributary, Malik Branch Canal and Hakara Branch Canal present a major defensive bulwark against possible Indian offensive design. On the flip side, the rapid expansion of population in both countries and infrastructure improvements close to the border areas have resulted in mushrooming of small towns and cities close to the border. The defence of these new townships now assumes importance.

The aforesaid indicates that at the micro-regional level, human activity has been a major agent to usher changes in terrain configuration. Geography thus can no longer be a barrier and can be altered to align with strategic requirements. There also emerges a requirement to constantly monitor geographical changes occurring in our neighbourhood and review our assessment of threat accordingly.

The Changing Time-Distance-Attribute Paradigm

The time-distance-attribute cube that defines geography has undergone a major change. Modern technology has made movement of people, goods and information faster than ever before. This has led to a new abstraction called 'Death of Distance' amplifying the diminishing relevance of geography in an interconnected world where not only has the time for physical movement reduced but passage of information is almost instantaneous. Advances in information technology have made borders irrelevant making the world function like a Global Village. The shrinking of the world that now provides an answer to 'anything, anytime and anywhere' is an antithesis to the 'something, sometime and somewhere' of the Old Age World. Distances have certainly lost their relevance in a world connected by high speed internet. This was evident to a large extent during the COVID pandemic that the world experienced from 2019-2021. Online classes, work from home, virtual meetings etc had indeed made the geographical cube of distance-time-attribute somewhat irrelevant. However, there is another way to look at the changes in physical geography being induced by man-made activities. It needs to be remembered that the geographical space or distance cannot be eliminated, only travel time between places can be reduced.

The defence enterprise is ripe with areas that are appropriate for application of technology. In recent years, most militaries are engaged in infusing technology to bolster their military capabilities. Robotics, Artificial Intelligence enabled weapon systems, military satellites, unmanned vehicles – aerial, surface and sub-surface, are the new order of the day. Modern armies are transforming from a 'manpower intensive' to a 'equipment intensive' force. It can be argued that advances in use of air power, mechanisation and development of ballistic missiles have overcome the impediments of geography and limitations of terrain to a large extent. Mechanisation has radically altered the 'time and distance' factor of a ground based operation. Air Borne and Air Transport operations can overcome natural and man-made obstacles. The concept of Air Land Battle incorporates the exploitation of third dimension for speeding up land operations. Long Range Vectors can accurately and effectively address targets in depth using advanced technology. However, to undertake such precise operations, intimate study of terrain has become even more important. Geographic technologies such as remote sensing, geographical information systems and location based services facilitate creating opportunities and employing other technologies. Technology is thus a facilitator and certainly cannot substitute geography, since accurate utility of technology in accomplishing strategic military objectives relies heavily on detailed knowledge of terrain. Integrating transformational technologies with geography's traditional strengths and diversity will pay dividends in the new age conflicts. It also needs to be understood that the geographical space between two places has not shrunk. This geographical space needs as much attention as in the past, or maybe more, in case one considers advances in technology related to camouflage and concealment. It is the travel time for vectors of choice that has altered. They are also more accurate and lethal. However, what has radically changed is the phenomenal reduction in time for observation, orientation, decision and action cycle to get completed and on the feedback cycle post the action.

The world has also been witness to the growing irrelevance of distance in some aspects of warfare demonstrated by US drone strikes being controlled from opposite end of the globe. Drones are, in the words of Tim Marshall, a clear example of technology overcoming some of the restrictions of geography – but at the same time they serve to underline geography's importance. The US houses its drones in at least fourteen bases around the world. The signal sent from the control station in US may need to travel through an underwater cable to Germany and then be sent up to a satellite belonging to a third country that sells bandwidth to the Pentagon. This is a reminder of the conceptual map of US power, which is needed in order to fully understand global geo-politics today.

Information warfare, a new domain of warfare that transcends into cyber warfare, electronic warfare and psychological operations may, on the face of it seem independent of geography. However, the same is not true in real sense. Cyber warfare is now viewed as a component of comprehensive national security rather than a stand-alone option. Information networks and vital computer systems of the adversary remain the targets. In the cyber space, while physical boundaries of nation states get blurred, the relevance of cyber geography in terms of networking infrastructure, location of critical gateways, traffic flows, location of data recovery centres, network operating centres etc become important. Electro-magnetic waves propagate in the atmosphere but interact with the physical elements of geography of a place through reflection and refraction. The siting of monitoring stations as part of electronic support measures or the power requirement of a jammer to a large extent, depend on physical geography and can be aided by latest geographical information system. Psychological warfare and influence operations, as subsets of information warfare have deep linkages with human geography. Information operations today can be viewed as a major non-kinetic method of warfare. Their impact on the human mind and perception can produce telling effects on the outcome of operations, change the desired end state and can even make the enemy capitulate before the battle.

Conventional operations of yesteryears were terrain centric. It required the enemy to be evicted from a piece of ground to proclaim victory. The battlefield comprised of a front, flank and rear. Asymmetric warfare or the fourth generation, as it is called, is an anti-thesis of conventional war. There is complete decentralisation of command and logistics chain. The order of battle of the adversary is not organised in hierarchical units. The whole organisation is amorphous. Terrorist organisations have little to do with tangible physical boundaries. In fact, the present wave of religious and transnational terrorism has no such geographical caging. This necessitates having an increased knowledge of both physical and human geographies of not only the affected regions but also forecast the likely trends of its spread. Approaching a socio-economic problem such as terrorism through a geographic lens leads to a greater understanding of not only locations of terrorist activities, but also social network connections, religious affinities, target objectives and social systemic operations.

The employment of armed forces is also expanding. Humanitarian Assistance and Disaster Relief (HADR) operations, Anti-Terrorist operations, Peace and Stabilisation Missions, either within the ambit of the United Nations (UN) or a regional grouping like the Shanghai Cooperation Organisation, are new order of the day. This involves study of military geography of areas beyond a nation's frontiers. Every nation hosts unique and distinct physical and human geography which makes undertaking of such operations a complex proposition. These extremes in geography require preparing for and adapting to variations in physical and human geography to enable prompt and smooth response during natural disasters and other contingencies.

Geo Information Systems

Geographic Information Systems or GIS today form the basis of war planning and execution. They are being utilized by military forces all over the world to gain an advantage over the adversaries. Recent advances have made it more efficient, accurate and the layered data on the digital maps provides more context. Information related to topography, elevation, water bodies, population, physical infrastructure, soil etc can be superimposed on the map in the form of layers thus aiding preparation and conduct of war.

In India, the PM Gati Shakti infrastructure plan for multi-modal connectivity brings together 16 ministries involved in execution of infrastructure projects. It provides comprehensive database of the ongoing and future projects integrated with 200 plus GIS layers which facilitates planning, designing and execution with a common vision. The connect to Geography is thus visible not only in military uses of GIS but also in the civil avenues.

As we transcend towards Data Centric Warfare, where we will aim for decision superiority, the amalgamation of new technologies like AI/ML and Big Data will give us multiple operational options. A refined GIS which is populated by multiple inputs will give us the much needed edge over our adversary.

Conclusion

Geography has been the most critical element in military planning over human evolution. Mackinder's Heartland Theory, Chanakya's Mandala Theory and Mahan's Sea Power Theory bear testament to the significance of various elements of geography at strategic and conceptual level. At the tactical and operational level, Shivaji's keen understanding of geography made him a successful ruler both in terms of fortress based defence, and use of terrain and people in offensive. Similarly, Swinton's "The Defence of the Duffer's Drift" illustrates the significance of this study at tactical level. Military Geography continues to have a pronounced impact on the nation's war effort despite an increasing role of technology and the same will continue in the future as well.

2

Geography as an Element in Strategy, Politics and Economics

"India's geography also encourages an insular outlook. It can be termed as an island nation by virtue of its peninsular shape which juts almost 2000 km into the Indian Ocean."

—By the author

General

The geography of India bestows on it attributes that not only contribute to its security but also facilitate commerce and trade. Located on the southern portion of the Asian heartland and yet separated from it by a chain of formidable mountain ranges, it is the ultimate 'Rimland' state. The peninsular shape of India jutting out into the Indian Ocean flanked by Arabian Sea to its West and the Bay of Bengal to its East, provides it a major maritime advantage. On its eastern frontiers the impregnable Jungles and mountains separating it from Myanmar, the Himalayas and Karakoram to the North and the Pamir and Hindu Kush to its northwest provide it security. Home to many ethnic groups with diverse linguistic and religious demography, the land was, for most part of its history, ruled by independent kings. The 'Idea of India - Bharatvarsh' as a political entity conforming to the geography of South Asia was for the first time encouraged by the advent of the Mauryan dynasty. The notion was sustained by subsequent rulers, prominent among them being the Guptas and Mughals.

India's geography also encourages an insular outlook. It can be termed as an island nation by virtue of its peninsular shape which juts almost 2000 km into the Indian Ocean. The lack of connectivity over the landmass results from the occupied and disputed territories as also the adversarial relations that India shares with Pakistan and China. Opportunities however, abound in the maritime domain as the peninsular shape gives us a dominating perch along the sea routes from East Africa to South East Asia. Stability and security in this region therefore has immense significance for India.

Historically, the geographical vulnerability of India lay on its northwest which provided access to India. It resulted in number of invasions from the times of Alexander to the Mongols (Turks, Afghans). The rise of sea faring nations in Europe and discovery of a sea route around the Cape of Good Hope heralded the arrival of European powers to India ostensibly in the garb of traders and merchants. It is ironic that the vast fleet of European ships were often guided by Indian merchant ships across the vast expanse of the Indian Ocean beyond the Cape of Good Hope. The British were able to outmaneuver the other powers and exploited the lack of unity among the Indian rulers to secure their rule over the country.

Geo-Politics

Nation states have always been unique in terms of their Physical and Human Geography, which bestows apposite status to them in regional politics and global affairs. However, in some cases, geography bestows disproportionately high importance to a region due to its strategic location. United States for example is the most secure nation from the perspective of conventional land as well as maritime threats. Its temperate climate is conducive to agriculture and its large landmass home to abundant natural resources. Its unhindered access to the Pacific and Atlantic Oceans provide it an opportunity to trade with Europe as well as Asia. On the other hand, Russia with its large landmass eminently qualifies to be a global power. However, a large portion of its landmass falls under the Artic-Tundra climate which is neither suitable for human habitation nor agriculture. Russia has a vast coast line but limited access to warm water ports. While the Arctic Ocean remains frozen for most of the year, the limited access that Russia enjoys to the Black Sea, the Baltic and the Sea of Japan, is vulnerable to getting choked in times of crisis. It is hence constrained in exercising influence commensurate to its gigantic size.

In modern times, the sea lines of communication (SLOCs) have emerged as major arteries for trade and transit. Unhindered access to the seas has been a major factor in the rise of global powers. Britain has unhindered access to the Atlantic and it was 'Great' till it had access to the Indian Ocean through colonies and acquisitions astride the Mediterranean (Gibraltar), Red Sea (Aden) and the South China Sea (Singapore). Presently its maritime reach is highly curtailed. Among the other European powers, France was always better placed than Germany with respect to access to the Mediterranean and the Atlantic. Land locked nations face a major strategic disadvantage due to lack of access to the sea and oceanic trade routes. This notwithstanding, there are regions which by virtue of their geographical location serve as a land bridge between geo-economic and geo-political power centres of importance. Central Asia was a land bridge that connected Asia to Europe. Along with East Europe, it was recognised by Halford John Mackinder, the famous 19th century geographer, as the Heartland in his famous essay, 'The Geographical Pivot of History', the possession of which was essential to gain influence and dominate the world.

Human geography has always played a vital role in determining the comprehensive national power of nations. The overwhelming presence of Hans in China's overall demographic profile is a source of major advantage to it. However, they are largely restricted to China's mainland. Ethnic Russians, courtesy the Soviet times, today have a significant presence in neighbouring countries like Ukraine, Belarus, Kazakhstan, Georgia etc. It provides a major leverage to Russia including the possibility of armed intervention, like the one exhibited in the seizing of the Crimean Peninsula from Ukraine in 2014, followed by the launch of special military operations in full scale invasion of Ukraine in 2022. The major conflicts around the globe today are mired along ethnic, religious and linguistic fault lines. This is in sharp contrast to territory centric conflicts of the previous century. Human geography and the current imbalance being caused due to migration is hence likely to be a major factor that will drive the course of global geo-politics.

Geo-Strategy

The strategic importance or vulnerability of a place to a large extent is determined by its physical geography and location. Nothing can be better illustrated than by the example of Turkey, a transcontinental country controlling overland trade routes between Europe and Asia. It also has access to Central Asia through the Caucasus, a region with which it shares its history, and in some regions, ethnic ties. The Mediterranean Sea connects it to North Africa also. The domination of the Bosphorus Strait and Agean Sea ensures that it can exercise intimate control over maritime movements that take place between The Mediterranean and the Black Sea. Even the website of Turkish Foreign Ministry claims that "The Afro-Eurasian geography Turkey is situated, at the epicenter, is an area where opportunities and risks interact in the most intimate way".

In the Indian context, Kashmir inspite of being besieged by insurmountable mountains and being landlocked in Northern India, provides a gateway through selected mountain passes, not only to Tibet but also to Afghanistan, Central Asia and Xinjiang through Ladakh. It was in the middle of the 19th century, located at a point, where the 'Three Empires Met'. Its control was hence important to imperial Britain not only during the era of expansionist Russia under its Czars but also after the communist takeover. Its importance to India has remained undiminished. The regaining of control over entire Kashmir will open up India's land routes to Central Asia through Afghanistan besides negating the possibility of Sino-Pakistan collusivity by removing the physical link between Pakistan and China. It also denies China the access to the Arabian Sea.

Location itself may bestow disproportionate importance to even very small countries. Djibouti, situated next to Bab-el-Mandeb, astride the world's busiest maritime trade route, enjoys a major geo-strategic advantage thus attracting all major global powers to establish a military base on its soil. But for its strategic location, it would have faced irrelevance similar to its neighbour Ethiopia. A similar importance arising out of geo-strategic location is enjoyed by Gibraltar, the British 'Rock' on the Southern tip of the Iberian Peninsula, which dominates the western approach into the Mediterranean Sea from the Atlantic Ocean. In the Indian context the Andaman Islands located astride the Ten Degree Channel that dominates the Malacca Straits assumes importance.

Geography bestows major vulnerabilities too. A prime example is the 'Siliguri Corridor' through which run the tenuous lines of communication between India and its North Eastern states. This geographical monstrosity was created due to the partition of India on its independence and has earned the epithet of a 'Chicken's Neck'. The carving out of a muslim majority East Pakistan disrupted India's physical and emotional links with the North East. Even the creation of Bangladesh in 1971 has not reduced Indian vulnerabilities entirely. In the present context, the vulnerability of the Corridor is accentuated by the historical proximity of the Chinese in the Chumbi Valley. The Siliguri Corridor remains India's foremost strategic vulnerability. In the same vein, the Straits of Malacca have been referred to as China's strategic dilemma by none other than Hu Jintao as bulk of China's out bound trade and inbound supplies of energy pass through these narrow Straits. The location of Andaman and Nicobar Islands astride the sea lanes to Malacca accentuates the Chinese vulnerability.

Geo-Economics

The economic potential of a state in terms of agricultural and industrial output and hence social development is once again to a large extent dependent on the geography of the region. It is not without reason that some countries are called as 'Bread Baskets' or 'Rice Bowls' of a region. On the other hand, some countries like China with a large land mass but limited arable land have always struggled to feed their huge population base. It is not without reason that Chinese investors are still scouting to lease farmlands in Africa and other parts of the globe besides engaging in illegal fishing in the IOR and Pacific, to bolster food security. Surface communication and connectivity influence trade and commerce, and consequently impact the region's geo-economy. In this regard, coastal nations, as brought out earlier, enjoy major advantages over land locked ones. This became pronounced as discovery of newer sea routes replaced ancient land avenues for trade and commerce. The famous Silk Route between China and the Mediterranean region was a popular overland trade route despite it passing through very treacherous and difficult terrain. It fell into disuse in the 8th Century after a sea route to Asia around the Cape of Good Hope was discovered. The discovery of this sea route initially led to the opening up of trade between Asian countries and maritime nations of Europe followed by eventual colonization of the former. For countries like India, it was a major setback as its feeder trade routes from North to the Silk Road dried up. In the South, the socio-cultural and religious influence that India exerted in South East Asia due to its maritime links was severed due to European dominance of the seas. Its maritime trade with Persian Gulf and West coast of Africa was also impacted. The sea route to the Indian Ocean around the Cape of Good Hope lost relevance once the Suez Canal was commissioned in 1869. The Suez Canal may lose some of its sheen in future as the Northern Sea Route (Polar Silk Route) with the melting of the Arctic ice, may connect Northern Europe and Russia to the Pacific and further to the Indian Ocean.

In contemporary times, India's Look East Policy evolved due to compulsions of geo-politics. Land locked on its West by an adversarial Pakistan and towards the North by an unfriendly China, also a strategic competitor, India was left with no choice but to look towards East in case it wishes to exploit the land route for access to the markets and resources of South East Asia.

Climate and Weather

It is well established that apart from terrain, climate also casts considerable influence on security related challenges faced by a region. Local population forms the first line of defence along the borders. Harsh climatic conditions affect population distribution. Areas like Ladakh, North Sikkim and

Arunachal are sparsely populated and security of borders in such areas poses a major challenge. It will not be out of place to mention that China started constructing a road through Aksai Chin to connect Sinkiang and Tibet in 1951 about which India came to know only in 1957 as the area was uninhabited besides being desolate and remote.

Climate and weather also accentuate logistics difficulties, especially for conduct of military operations. The South-Western monsoon was a crucial factor that led to the postponement of India's offensive to liberate Bangladesh in 1971. While Prime Minister Smt Indira Gandhi desired an Indian intervention in the month of April, General Sam Manekshaw wanted time to build up stocks and for the monsoon to get over. In hindsight, the lightning campaign would have been difficult to conclude in just fourteen days if it was undertaken during the monsoons. In the 1962 conflict, the Chinese having captured areas upto foothills in Kameng sector and south of the McMahon Line in some other valleys, decided to declare a unilateral ceasefire and withdraw across the watershed not for military or political considerations but due to the impending winters which may have witnessed their forces stranded South of the snow bound watershed without any logistic support.

The impact of weather on military operations is felt not only at the strategic level but even at the tactical level. During the 1947-48 operations in Uri Sector of the Kashmir valley, Indian troops captured features of Ledi Gali and Pir Kanthi, both located in high altitude on the Pir Panjal Ranges, at a considerable cost. These features, however had to be abandoned in winters, due to the extremely high level of snowfall that the Pir Panjal range usually experiences. The northwestern slopes of these ranges receive more sunshine causing early melting of snows from the Pakistani side. This simple yet recurring phenomenon assisted Pakistan to occupy Ledi Gali and Pir Kanthi without a fight next year, much before the snow could melt on the Indian side.

Ladakh remains inaccessible during winters due to closure of the Zojila pass and the Rohtang axis for which stocking needs to be carried out during summers not only for the troops stationed there but also for the civil population. The region being physically cut off is consequently vulnerable during winters but even as the winter ebbs, the vulnerability of the region rises due to depleted stock levels. To overcome the challenges of weather and climate, every year the Indian Army resorts to what is called 'winter stocking' along the Northern borders and 'monsoon stocking' in the North East. It is a logistic exercise India is compelled to undertake every year. The altitude and weather of a place also impose severe restrictions on stationing of troops. Depending on the altitude of their employment, troops have to undergo acclimatisation – a process that ranges from 6 to 14 days. Even tourists who arrive in Leh (altitude of 11000 feet) are advised rest on day one so that they can get accustomed to the rarified atmosphere. It is not without reason that military operations in mountains are called a logistician's nightmare.

Conclusion

While geography bestows upon nations strategic leverage or vulnerability, it is the exploitation of the geographical advantage that leads to incidents of geo political significance thus contributing to creation of history itself. It is well known that the formidable Himalayas along the Northern frontiers of India have provided security to the Indian sub-continent for centuries whereas the open plains of Punjab were passage of periodic invasions mostly through the Khyber Pass. Examples of current history may be more relevant. The physical occupation of Siachen Glacier by India in 1984 created a wedge which negated the possibility of Sino-Pak collusivity manifesting from within the erstwhile state of Jammu and Kashmir. This was a major strategic move by India. In 1999, Pakistan attempted to exploit the strategic vulnerability of Srinagar-Leh National Highway, our major communication artery connecting Leh, by occupying heights in Drass and Kargil sectors through which it could intimately dominate the National Highway by both observation and fire. The counter measures undertaken by the Indian Army to evict the intruders resulted in the famous Kargil conflict. Similarly, the occupation of North Doklam in Bhutan by the PLA in 2017 was not without purpose. The aim was to have permanent Chinese presence closer to the Siliguri

Corridor. The Chinese intrusion would have inched forward up to the Jampheri Ridge had Indian Army not intervened.

The influence of geography over history has been well documented. The rational options available to a state in times of crisis get either augmented or limited by its geography. Since physical geography to a large extent remains unalterable, the strategic options available to nations in times of crisis will be finite. Hence it will not be out of context to conclude that even the strategic trajectory of a region can be predicted with reasonable accuracy by a careful analysis of its geography. The same holds true for economic predictions. No wonder the word 'geography' precedes politics and economics in words like Geo-Politics, Geo-Strategy and Geo-Economics. It is true for Geo-Strategy also where geography forms an invaluable and indispensible part of any strategic formulation from Grand Strategy, Military Strategy to even a 'Theatre Strategy'.

3

Ancient Indian Wisdom and Its Relevance in Modern Strategy & Statecraft

> *"The India Way rests on ancient wisdom to address contemporary challenges. It combines traditional values with modern strategy, drawing from history while innovating for the future. This approach not only enhances our global standing but also ensures our national interests are protected."*
>
> —FM Dr Jaishankar

Introduction

In recent times, the Army Training Command (ARTRAC) and the College of Defence Management (CDM) released several publications on 'Ancient Indian Stratagems'. Concurrently, the Indian Army launched "Project Udbhav" in collaboration with the United Services Institution of India (USI) to "research on indigenous military systems to integrate age-old wisdom with modern military pedagogy". Just as it happens with most novel and radical ideas and initiatives, a controversy erupted with some academics delving into military affairs and veterans stating that in the age of nuclear war and AI-dominated net-centric operations, there was no place for ancient wisdom. It was their opinion that military weapons & systems, supporting tactics and military organisations have undergone such a transformative change that ancient stratagems are no longer applicable, not even the enduring principles of warfare. An extreme view was that Udbhav was part of the decolonising effect of the Amritkaal.

This chapter, therefore, is an attempt to address the larger question: are tenets of ancient stratagems and wisdom such as Kautilya's

'Arthashastra', Thiruvalluvar's Thirukkural or from other countries such as Sun Tzu's Art of War still applicable to modern war and warfighting?

Warfare and Society

We are all aware that the character of warfare evolves and transforms continuously with time, marked by technological advancements and the changing geo-political and geo-economic landscape. War has moved from being fought between organised tribes to feudal armies of agrarian societies to the armed Forces of an industrialised world to now becoming multi-protagonist wars fought in a globalised and interconnected world. This has blurred the lines between state and non-state actors while advancements in technology have led to precision targeting and remote warfare capabilities. Furthermore, several new domains of warfare have emerged, in addition to the conventional domains of land, air and maritime such as space, cyber and electromagnetic (EM) spectrum. Increasing reliance on information and psychological operations has transformed the battlefield into a multidimensional arena.

It is often said that technology has changed the character of war but its basic nature remains unchanged. The nature of the war is violent and destructive. Some also say that 'wars' have ceased to exist today. That is also true. The kind of declared wars we witnessed during World War II and previous centuries do not exist anymore. However, Conflict still exists. Competition, Crisis, Confrontation, Conflict and Combat – these 5Cs all exist together as part of a single continuum.

All these Cs arise out of the basic human nature of 'Self Protection' and 'Dominance'. The interplay between man, society and nature leads to the 5Cs. Hence, ancient concepts, precepts and principles remain timeless. They are as relevant today as they were in the past. Only the presentation or format keeps evolving.

Development of Strategic Thoughts

A civilisation's strategic thoughts are shaped by various factors such as geography and historical experiences. The Indian civilisation derives its strength from over 5,000 years of heritage. Countless lessons from Indian history serve as the foundation for Indian strategic thinking. The Indian civilisation, among the oldest in the world, has consistently sought excellence. Looking back at the Mauryan empire of the fourth and third centuries BCE, we find an ideal example of a state navigating the complex geo-political situation of that time to survive and flourish. The Mauryan empire, which covered almost all of present-day India, had a vast and effective administrative structure that supported a central authority and encouraged loyalty. It was governed by a robust "nationalistic" policy, which had a mix of idealism and realism factored into it. The tenets of this are enshrined in the treatise of Arthashastra. The subsequent empires of the Guptas and Cholas do provide a precedent for Indian political unity and a pervasive common strand of strategic thought and culture. A closer examination of our history, account of battles, and thoughts of the politico-military leadership that led the nation during those times is, therefore, essential. Some of these pearls of ancient wisdom may flow from general governance or administration, while some may be part of ancient parables and folklore. The existing literature needs to be examined for its relevance in current times.

Ancient Indian Stratagems

The ancient Indian stratagems detailed in texts like the Ramayana, Mahabharata, Bhagavad Gita, Arthashastra, Nitisara, Panchatantra and Thirukural and several others encapsulate these strategic thoughts and serve as repositories of knowledge. These ancient texts also feature intricate narratives of warfare where rulers and strategists employed a diverse array of stratagems to navigate complex situations. Furthermore, these texts delve into broad themes of ethics, morality and the consequences of war, providing timeless lessons in effective decision-making and conflict resolution.

The annals of ancient Indian history are replete with examples of strategies where deceptive manoeuvres, psychological warfare and skilful use of terrain were employed to outwit adversaries. Indian rulers utilised deception by disguising troop movements and employing ruse to confuse their adversaries. The Arthashastra broadly describes two types of espionage, i.e. sansthah or stationary spies and sancharah or roaming spies. The stationary spies included false disciples (kapatikas), recluses (udasthitas), householders (grihapatika), merchants (vaidehakas), and ascetics (tapas). The wandering spies included students (satris), desperados (tikashnas), and poisoners (rasadas). Women were recommended as spies in the wandering group. They were deployed as mendicants (bhikshukis), wandering nuns (parivrajikas), shavelings (mundas), and courtesans (vrishalis). Psychological tactics were employed to demoralise foes through intimidation or sowing seeds of discord within their ranks. It would not be wrong to take the example from the Mahabharata. Shalya, the maternal uncle of Nakul and Sahdev, join Kauravas, because of pure deceit. Shri Krishna gets a promise out of him saying you won't betray us. As a result, you find him being with Karna, as his charioteer, but one who constantly undermines him, irrespective of his achievements. Similarly, during the Kurukshetra battle, the Pandavas resorted to tactical deception by falsely claiming the demise of Ashwatthama, exploiting the emotional vulnerability of Guru Dronacharya. This strategic manoeuvre contributed to Dronacharya's momentary disheartenment and subsequent vulnerability, leading to his defeat. Tactical retreats were strategically executed to lure the enemy into vulnerable positions or to conserve resources for counterattacks. Exploiting favourable terrain such as high ground or chokepoints formed an integral part of ancient warfighting techniques. Additionally, dividing enemies by exploiting internal divisions or forming alliances weakened larger adversaries. Magadha's war with Vaishali and the rise of Chandragupta Maurya featured the use of kutayuddha including the use of spies and assassins. Economic warfare tactics such as disrupting supply lines or capturing resources, further undermined the enemy's capacity to wage war.

Several Ancient Literatures such as Dhanurveda, and the epics of Mahabharata and Ramayana highlight the use of advanced weapons such as Pashupatiastra, Nagastra, Garudastra, Brahamastra, and Narayanastra, that greatly impacted the outcomes of battles. While their relevance in today's context needs examination and analysis, the basic precepts and principles remain relevant. Some of them are explained in succeeding paragraphs.

Just War or the Righteous War

Western literature credits the first advocation of "Just War" (bellum iustum)' to Saint Augustine in the 4th Century. The Just War theory is a doctrine of Military ethics that aims to ensure that war is morally justifiable. The concept is based on two cardinal postulates i.e. ethical conduct during the war (jus in bello) and the right to go to war (jus ad bellum).

The concept of 'Just War' has existed in India since ancient times in the form of 'Righteous War' and with 'Righteous Conduct'. Lord Ram was an early progenitor of this concept. In the epic Ramayana, Lord Ram had every right to go to war and he and his army demonstrated ethical conduct during the war. The vanquished, unlike in other civilisations, were not exterminated. One of their clans, Vibhisana, was anointed as the king and the captured territories were returned. Lord Rama returned to his territory in Ayodhya. Even in Mahabharata, the Pandavas were the aggrieved party, victims of attempted assassination and an unfair partition of their kingdom, in addition to their woman being insulted. They were justified to go to war.

War Termination

Securing victory in a war does not guarantee enduring peace. This is evident in most modern conflicts where violence continues even after the war has come to an end due to the absence of a well-thought-out exit strategy. Sustaining stability requires the humility of the victor. An inclusive approach towards the future involving both the conqueror and the defeated is imperative. A stable conclusion to the war is of paramount importance as it results in enduring peace.

In both the epics, Mahabharata and the Ramayana, the end game demonstrates a well-thought-out Exit Strategy. Sri Krishna employed multiple measures to bring about a stable conclusion to the war. In modern parlance, they could be referred to as 'war termination' and 'consolidation operations'. Krishna and the Pandavas not only interacted with the Kauravas but also engaged with their allies after the war, incorporating them into the decision-making process for the future. Despite their years of rule, the Pandavas never harboured ill feelings towards the allies of the Kauravas.

Balance of Power and Statecraft

Kautilya's Mandala theory is a timeless lesson on the 'Balance of Power'. Kautilya used the shape of Mandal to develop a political geometry of concentric circles to explain the relationship between 12 different types of kingdoms and their kings. The central reference point was own king who was referred to as the 'Vijigishu' (meaning the conqueror or the ambitious king). This theory propounds the wisdom of forming alliances which is also referred to as the Sukraniti. The epic Mahabharata is once again a lesson in statecraft, diplomacy and balance of power. Rulers and Kingdoms get aligned to two opposing poles in a pre-war environment much like during the Cold War of yesteryears or even the uncertain and VUCA environment of today.

Another lesson enshrined in Mahabharata is the soft power of diplomacy, advice and wise counsel. The military power of Lord Krishna's Yadava Kingdom went to Kauravas. Lord Krishna's sage advice was able to shape the balance of power in favour of the Pandavas who eventually emerged victorious after 18 days of Mahabharat in Kurukshetra.

Net Assessment and Strategy

It took more than a millennium for the Western world to formalise the process of Net Assessment. Ancient Indian texts spoke about its application in the formulation of national strategies. Kautilya's Shadgunya Niti or the six forms of state policy, has explained them as Treaty – Making (Samadhi), War (Vigraha), Observing Neutrality (Asana), Marching (Yana), Making Alliance (Samsraya) and Simultaneous Policy of Peace and Hostility (Dwadibhav). The Saptanga theory is a lesson in evaluating Comprehensive National Power (CNP). The seven pillars of a Nation-state are the Swami (the king), Amatya (the ministers), Janapada (the territory), Durg (a fortified capital), kosha (the treasury), Dand (system of Justice or force) and Mitra (friend).

Arthashastra also brings to the fore the importance of convergence of the three elements of battlecraft craft namely strength (men, material and resources), time (weather, darkness) and place (high altitude, far seas, choke points, jungles) for maximising the impact of one's military strength. These strategies, originating thousands of years ago, continue to hold relevance today as the international behaviour of nations, rooted in human nature, remains unaltered.

Multi-Alignment

India's tradition of being "Vishwabandhu" or a friend to the world, has roots in ancient times and remains a fundamental aspect of its foreign policy. Throughout history, India has upheld principles of peace, cooperation and non-interference in the affairs of other nations. This approach is evident in all ancient Indian texts particularly the Arthashastra, Nitisara and the Thirukurral, that advocate for diplomacy, alliances and economic ties to ensure national security and prosperity. India's engagement with the world has historically been characterised by cultural exchange, trade and spiritual diplomacy, fostering goodwill and mutual understanding. Even during periods of conflict, India has sought peaceful resolutions and prioritised regional stability. By promoting global peace, sustainable development, and mutual respect, Bharat has always strived to be a responsible global actor, honouring its ancient tradition of being a 'Vishwabandhu'.

Internal Security

In contrast to Western concepts of national security, ancient Indian wisdom places greater emphasis on internal security. The vulnerability of a state was perceived to be greater when its political legitimacy was weak, surpassing the susceptibility of a state with a smaller military force. Kautilya proposes a solution to quell internal disturbances by either winning over dissenting leaders or addressing the underlying causes of discontent, aiming to alleviate grievances against the government. In the event of rebellion, rulers should employ means such as conciliation, gifts and dissension; avoiding the use of force against their people as it is deemed unlikely to produce the intended results and may, instead, result in undesirable repercussions. Kautilya surmises that "The best fortress is to be found in the love of the people, for although you may have fortresses, they will not save you if you are hated by the people".

He had also indicated that "a mole within is worse than a sore outside" highlighting that it takes only one insider at the right place to corrupt the whole system. To control the internal fault lines, a vast network of spies to deal with various subjects of state security, including corruption as outlined in the Arthashastra. Thirukkural also cautions against internal enemies, underscoring their capacity to pose threats, particularly during moments of crisis. It says "A house with internal enmity fades, as iron when filed crumbles".

This aligns with the contemporary focus on internal stability. We have learnt that the biggest threat to a nation-state is not from external aggression but from internal strife. External aggressions unite people, whereas, it is the internal turmoil that often results in demographic fissures and persistent unrest. These ancient pearls of wisdom reinforce the requirement for nation-states to deal with internal disturbances firmly.

Importance of Military Intelligence

Military Intelligence serves as a crucial tool for effective strategising. Ancient Indian wisdom highlights the significance of intelligence and operations guided by intelligence. It emphasises the ability to analyse the information received from various sources. While we may possess satellites and other systems for information gathering, the ultimate achievement lies in the capability to analyse and decipher the inputs and therefore the plans of the adversary. According to ancient Indian texts, it is essential not only to keep adversaries under surveillance but also to monitor employees and kinsmen. In Mahabharata, Krishna recognised the pivotal role of intelligence, not only in the execution of operations but also in shaping the battlefield and the overall environment before, during and after the war. This accentuates the strategic value of well-informed decision-making and planning in the realm of military engagements.

Tactical Maneuvers

These epics and ancient literature also contain many tactical frameworks such as the 'Vyuha Rachna – Dharm'. Agni Purana, probably, is one of the oldest literature that propounds the philosophy of 'Reserves on the battlefield', a concept that has become an integral part of modern-day armies. The importance of Fort (Durg) and Army (Dand) can be understood at the operational level where there is a need for a strong pivot or firm base (Fort) and a mobile arm or force (Army) for the conduct of war. The Sam (Kosha) is the economic well-being. The killing of Bali by Lord Rama, and Arjuna's killing of Bhishma with the help of Shikhandi or Yudhishthir calling out Ashwathama's name are in some ways depictions of deception in our ancient texts. These tactical-level deceptions were possibly permitted towards the overall strategic aim of upholding the Dharma.

Conclusion

There is no denying that the broad stratagems on warfare enumerated in the ancient Indian texts provide invaluable foundational knowledge about the 'Principles of Warfare' and remain relevant to date. These, however, may not find applications towards the postulation of real-time 'Tactics, Techniques and Procedures (TTPs)' for contemporary and Modern Warfare. Our ancient wisdom is a fount of motivation and inspiration for us. It reminds us that powerful nations build narratives and others follow. India was a 'Vishwa Guru' once and in today's age, aspires to be a 'Vishwa Mitra'. The ancient wisdom stored in parables, stratagems, quotes and mythology remains relevant in understanding larger dimensions of strategy. They also helped to dispel the West-cultivated narrative that Indians lacked strategic culture.

Modern India's conduct in the international realm has followed a unique trajectory, often defying the tenets of the dominant theories on International Relations. India's conceptualisation of the tenets of National

Security and calibration of relations with friends and foes in the pursuit of national interest highlight our strategic behaviour, characteristically Indian. A deeper analysis of the ancient Indian strategic culture and its relevance to modern-day strategic thinking and leadership would greatly assist us in seeking solutions to contemporary strategic challenges.

Our position in the comity of nations and thus our stakes in international affairs stem from our heritage. It reflects our deep-rooted strategic and cultural characteristics. These unique identities, traits and behaviours form the core characteristics of the civilisation and its successful existence. This holds particular significance for civilisations like India, which have experienced numerous upheavals in its history, including periods of foreign rule. The strength of our rich civilisation brought with it a sense of responsibility towards all of humanity. The evolving challenges in today's national security necessitate that systems and processes supporting strategic planning remain consistently relevant and applicable. While establishing cultural identity through the study of ancient knowledge is crucial, it is equally important to extract relevant lessons and subject them to the scrutiny of modern thought for practical application.

4

National Security: A Conceptual Framework

> *"National security is not merely about protecting physical borders; it involves safeguarding the cultural, economic, and social fabric of the nation."*
>
> —NSA Ajit Doval

Introduction

Nation is a concept denoting a common ethnic and cultural identity. It promotes emotional relationships among the people constituting the nation. The notion of a nation is abstract, largely associated with people whereas a country is associated with land, which is tangible. It may also create a bond as strong as that of a nation in people who live in that geography.

The physical attribute of geography being added to the idea of a nation has evolved into the concept of a nation-state. It is a recent construct and is a fusion of a nation with a state. A state is a political unit defined in terms of territory whereas a nation, as stated earlier, is associated with a group of people or a race. A nation-state provides formal recognition and political legitimacy to the geography and the people who reside in it, as a nation. It provides a legal framework for governance for the citizens of the nation-state. The glue that binds a nation is common beliefs, shared history and aspirations of a better collective future. In a nation-state, the aspirational aspect of a better and secure future is performed by structures created for the governance of the nation-state.

The three basic constituents of a modern nation-state are its territory, its people and its ideology. The state is duty-bound to protect all three and it does so by creating various instruments like the armed forces, intelligence organisations, law enforcement agencies, disaster response mechanisms etc besides structures for governance and administration. The government that presides over the nation-state also identifies issues that will further the cause of its people and its ideology. These can be termed as national interests. National interests can thus translate into aspirations, ambitions and goals which revolve around political, economic, cultural and security needs with national security being the most fundamental. They have a wider perspective and amount to the total of all national values. Core interests are a subset of national interests and are somehow related to the three main constituents of a nation-state.

Aim

The framework that furthers the national interests and mitigates the threats and challenges to a nation-state may be broadly called the National Security Strategy. This chapter aims to share a perspective on the development of a Strategy for National Security under the conceptual framework of its architecture, ingredients, policy and processes.

Responsibilities of a Nation-State

The safeguarding of sovereignty and maintenance of its territorial integrity is the first major responsibility of a nation-state. Next is the protection of its people which includes the diaspora residing outside the boundaries of the state. The ideology of a state is a set of political beliefs that lay the blueprint for a social order. In brief, the ideology of a state can be defined in terms of core values that are generally enshrined in the Constitution of the state.

National Security

National Security is the capacity of a state to overcome conventional and sub-conventional threats that endanger its territorial integrity and sovereignty, and the well-being of its people. It also undertakes measures to mitigate the challenges the nation-state may face in future while trying to protect its territory, people and ideology. While the concept of national security was initially predicated around territoriality and defending a sovereign territory from armed aggression, today it includes non-military dimensions like economic security, energy security, food security, cyber security etc. In these domains, the threats posed by other nation-states as well as non-state actors are included. The expanded scope of national security thus includes protection against non-traditional threats like ecology, environment and climate change. Trans-national non-traditional threats like illegal immigration, human trafficking, gun running and narcotics trade are some man-made challenges that can also be included in the ambit of national security.

The threats are imminent. They require immediate action to neutralise. Challenges have a longer gestation period and will require a different strategy for mitigation. Opportunities are difficult to predict but may provide maximum benefit to the constituents of the nation-state. A nation-state should also be poised to seize opportunities that present themselves for furtherance of its goals.

The security of a nation-state involves many facets. Its architecture can be visualised as three concentric circles. The outermost circle addresses the problem of how to secure the nation-state, the middle circle relates to issues concerning the defence of a nation-state and the inner circle denotes the military preparedness of the nation-state. An all-round analysis of these could translate into a National Security Strategy (NSS), a National Defence Strategy (NDS) and a National Military Strategy (NMS). Service Specific Strategies may flow and follow from it. The three concentric circles looking at securing a nation, defending a nation and military preparedness of a nation, seamlessly contribute to each other.

Figure 1: The Three Concentric Circles of National Security Architecture

Securing a Nation State

The global security environment is marked by uncertainty and global peace is under more stress than ever before. In an increasingly interconnected world, no nation can remain immune to conflicts and contestations, even if they occur outside national boundaries or areas of interest. The security of a nation-state is a complex enterprise. A state seeks to progressively achieve higher levels of national security, which gives it a continuous and ceaseless character. With the remit of national security being larger, one has to take a long-term view of the global and regional security environment affecting the territory, people, and ideology of a nation-state to secure it.

Territorial Integrity

Human civilisation has evolved over land and disputes over territory between tribes, kingdoms and modern nation-states are a part of our civilisational history. Sovereignty over land is absolute and national boundaries, once recognised, are easy to protect. Sovereignty in airspace is an extension of land and infringements are at best, of a temporary nature. Sovereignty in the maritime domain is nebulous as passage through even territorial waters is not considered an infringement of sovereignty. Extension of the maritime domain to underwater and seabed (minerals and communication cables) complicates the issue of ownership and sovereignty. Open seas and oceans are, of course, global commons for equal use by all nation-states. Space too is considered a global common for use by all. In an interconnected global world, national territories sometimes extend to include overseas (colonial) possessions, occupied territories, and military bases acquired or taken on lease agreements. Economic interests and investments in third countries sometimes affect the food and energy security of the nation leasing the territory, adding a new dimension to national interests vis-à-vis territorial sovereignty. Competing interests of nation-states in third countries complicate matters further. Securing territorial interests may not be singularly achievable owing to the associated complexities and may need partnerships and alliances with other like-minded nations against common challenges or threats, while force structures for maintaining the sovereignty over land, air, maritime and newly emerging domains can be created. Equally important is to develop concepts to maintain national interests in nebulous domains and uncharted territories. It may also extend to the realm of intelligence-sharing networks and organisations for early warning as well as to technologies that help warfighting.

People

The concept of a nation creates an emotional bond between people even if they reside in different states under a different governance system. Their security and safety have at times become a cause of inter-state conflicts. Another extreme of this is people of one state voluntarily working and residing in different countries. Such people contribute to the economic activity and GDP of both nations. The well-being of such nationals remains a matter of concern for the home state of those individuals. The security of the Indigenous diaspora becomes a complex matter when they work for governments of other nations, multi-national corporations and international organisations as they are governed by the policies and rules of that country or organisation. Migration of population and citizenship issues also complicate governance and national security. Protecting the citizens of a nation-state may be simple but providing security to the people of a nation is a major challenge, especially in a globally interconnected world. This will require a creative approach, especially for a country like India which has a large workforce working across the state.

Ideology

Radical ideologies and divergent narratives are creating new fissures in societies and nation-states. Religious, cultural and ethnic fault lines are being exploited due to the immense penetration of internet-driven social media. No nation-state can remain immune to the effects of the rise of radical ideologies, religious sentiments, xenophobic tendencies, separatism and violent extremism. These developments pose significant challenges to modern nation-states and more so to multi-cultural and multi-religious societies and states like India. A democratic society values its citizens more than the state. The ultimate sovereignty of a state rests with the people. Individual identity and ideology were important as a concept but have now found a new voice through electronic and social media. Individual and group ideologies have the potential to disturb the social fabric and are a major challenge to national security for most modern and democratic nation-states. Today it is possible to penetrate networks that control the flow of information and hence target the minds of the people thus weakening a nation-state through influence operations. Such a strategy to weaken a nation being insidious can be run over an extended time horizon. It becomes imperative for a nation-state to create narratives, manage perceptions and carry out social re-engineering, not only for our population but also for our friends, allies and adversaries alike. This is therefore the most complex domain of national security.

The security of a modern nation-state is thus complex and requires more than just mitigating the threats and challenges to its three main constituents. Other important factors that have a major impact on national security are as follows:

- ***Technology.*** Science and technology are critical for the development of a nation-state and one of the arenas where its impact is felt the most is war and warfare. It is required not only for the security of a nation-state but also for the socio-political development and economic prosperity of the state. Technological advancements fundamentally reshape national security strategies by enhancing both offensive and defensive capabilities. Innovations in cybersecurity, artificial intelligence, quantum computing and surveillance technologies enable states to protect critical infrastructure and gain intelligence superiority. For instance, AI-driven analytics can predict and mitigate threats in real time, while quantum encryption offers unprecedented communication security. On the offensive side, cyber warfare tools can disrupt adversary networks and operations without conventional military engagement. Moreover, emerging technologies such as hypersonic weapons and autonomous drones redefine strategic deterrence and power projection. Therefore, one has to keep an eye on and continuously scan and monitor the global ecosystem as well as push domestic innovators and technologists to create, integrate and advance technologies, ensuring a balance between leveraging technological advantages and mitigating vulnerabilities.

- ***Economic Prosperity.*** It may include issues like energy security, trade, manufacturing and services etc. Gross Domestic Product (GDP) growth again contributes to the security of the state by enhancing the defence budget and ensuring the economic well-being of the citizens. A robust economy attracts foreign investments, which can be leveraged to enhance technological infrastructure and defence capabilities. Strong trade relations ensure access to critical resources and markets reducing vulnerability to economic coercion. Manufacturing growth not only creates jobs but also establishes a resilient supply chain for defence materials, diminishing reliance on imports. The services sector, particularly in technology and information services, fosters innovation essential for modern defence systems. Overall, sustained GDP growth enables a nation to allocate greater resources to its defence budget, thereby enhancing military readiness and the welfare of its citizens.

- ***Partnerships and Alliances.*** Historically, like-minded nations have aligned together to face common threats and challenges or to serve the larger interests of a nation. These have generally evolved into formal treaties that are legally binding as per the terms agreed upon. Partnerships may not have a binding security or military dimension attached to them but convey a general convergence of national interests. In an interconnected global world, nation-states look at collective security, whether economic or military. The European Union (EU) and the North Atlantic Treaty Organisation (NATO) are examples of treaty organisations. Non-alignment is an alternate means to provide security to a nation-state, especially in a world that is divided into major power blocs. Formal alliances do impinge upon the sovereignty of a state and hence there is a tradeoff between the nature of security a state may seek vis-a-vis the sovereignty it is ready to surrender.
- ***Arms Control and Disarmament.*** Chemical, biological, radiological and nuclear (CBRN) threats affect the whole human race. These global threats impact international security and as its subset, the national security of a nation-state. Issues like the proliferation of Weapon of Mass Destruction (WMD) technologies and the possibility of these falling into the hands of non-state actors further add to the security challenge. Cooperation between states in military matters, especially in the realms of elimination, reduction and limiting of such weapons will result in a cooperative security regime with regulatory means to thwart such security threats. An alternate view on arms control is that it is a means to deny a capability that few nation-states have already weaponised. A nuanced view of arms control and disarmament is hence needed.

Defence of a Nation State

It is a subset of National Security with its remit being larger than the application of military force. It looks at instruments that may defend the nation without the application of military force and strategic planning for the application of military force if it has to be used. Apart from tangible instruments of power, there is an abstract element of developing a strategic mindset amongst the citizens of a nation-state. There can be many lines of action through which one can enhance the capability of a state to defend itself. A few of these are being discussed in subsequent paragraphs.

Capability Building and Sustenance

The efficacy of any armed force depends on two basic requirements. These are the sustenance of the force to counter present-day threats and capability building for future challenges. While sustenance voids may have to be made up through the import of weapons, ammunition, spares and equipment, the capability building should preferably be indigenous. This will insulate the nation-state against any disruptions due to global geo-political events or even pandemics like COVID-19. Till the time indigenous capabilities are developed, a nation-state may have to resort to striking a balance between imported and indigenous technologies and equipment, ensuring that adequate stocks are maintained at all times to cater for a prolonged conflict or to ensure a timely surge in capacity.

Defence Research and Development (R&D)

For the indigenous capacity building to take place, there will be a requirement for indigenisation of import substitutes and innovation when it comes to the development of new products, systems and technologies. Defence R&D will be vital for both. Nation-states will have to resort to partnerships and joint ventures with foreign equipment manufacturers to obtain technologies for indigenisation. It will serve the dual purpose of achieving self-reliance and also reduce the import burden, thus giving more opportunities to a nation-state to sustain itself. Indigenisation in Defence is critical to national security as it keeps the technological expertise intact and encourages spin-off technologies which lead to innovation. For innovation, the user, the academia, the private industry and the government will have to collaborate towards technology development. Such technologies developed indigenously, being tailor-made, will yield better chances of success.

Defence Manufacturing

A technologically strong and resilient manufacturing sector is vital for Defence and national security in more than one way. Without the domestic sector having the capability to produce strategically important defence equipment, the ability of the nation to defend itself will be vulnerable to foreign influence. Critical infrastructure, advanced technologies, applications and other such strategic industries also rely on a strong domestic manufacturing base for economic stability and security. It also ensures the resilience of supply chains and logistics. When considering the defence and security of a nation, it is important to invest in cutting-edge technologies to keep manufacturing competitive, resilient, efficient and secure. A strong and proven defence manufacturing sector will be capable of providing support to other desirous and friendly nations too. Defence exports will thus generate revenue for the nation's economy, which has an impact on national security.

Defence Diplomacy

Defence diplomacy does not have a universally accepted definition, which allows nation-states to modify and utilise it for their own security needs. It is referred to as a 'Powerful Tool of Statecraft' and describes the non-violent use of military force to achieve national objectives by conducting activities like training exercises, the establishment of training teams for the capacity building of the host nation, cultural exchanges, etc. In recent years, defence diplomacy has developed as a significant player on the global politico-military stage to create partnerships, strengthen ties with allies or demonstrate one's might to an adversary. It contributes to the shaping and implementation of the security policy and foreign policy of nation-states.

Strategic Culture

Every nation has its own set of decision-makers, be it from the government, the military or a mix of both. Strategic culture is the set of beliefs, customs and traditions held by these strategic decision-makers about the political objective of war and the most effective ways of achieving it. It decides how the nation-state utilises its resources to meet its end goals. The citizens and the society in a nation must understand the importance of security in all its dimensions, be it external, internal, economic or social. A Strategic Culture will have to be created in the nation to create awareness among the people on the 'whole of nation' approach that is sine qua non to counter emerging challenges.

Defence Budget

The security paradigm for a nation-state has to be constantly reviewed in light of the threats and challenges which keep evolving. The defence of the nation is ensured by a strong, modern and capable army which is equipped to respond to any and every contingency that the nation may have to face. The defence budget is utilised for sustaining and provisioning the current force as well as for its capability building.

Civil-Military Fusion

This ensures the optimal utilisation of civil and military resources to achieve national objectives. It fuses military professionalism with political ideologies. The infusion of state-of-the-art technologies across multiple domains lends further credence to the concept of civil-military fusion. The development of dual-use technologies and infrastructure optimises resources. Civil-military fusion is paramount for the security of the citizens during Humanitarian Assistance and Disaster Management operations.

Military Preparedness

Military security is the capability of a nation-state to deter aggression and defend itself. A nation-state also can enforce its policy choices through military force. Both need military preparedness, which lies at the very core of the three concentric circles that have been discussed earlier. Just like the strength of the entire structure is based on the strength of the core, the strength of national security, the foundation of defence of a nation, depends on the strength of its military preparedness. In a democratic setup, the military is always 'an instrument of last resort'. The military should, therefore, never fail. Military preparedness primarily remains a function of the Armed Forces which are entrusted with the responsibility of preserving the territorial integrity and protecting the people and the ideology of the nation-state. They have to have both the deterrence value as also the capability to wage war if needed. Commencing with the development of strategies, concepts and doctrines, military preparedness progresses to 'force generation' and creates options for 'force employment'. The ambit of military preparedness, however, spreads beyond the preparation or conduct of war. Some important aspects are:

- The Armed Forces are responsible for the safety of the national diaspora when they are outside the geography of the nation. Evacuation of these citizens from a warzone or conflict zone is undertaken by the armed forces. Such operations are called Non-Combatant Evacuation Operations and need specific capabilities which the military must be prepared for. It also needs cohesion between the diplomacy and the military.
- With an increase in connectivity, nation-states today have their economic interests based outside their geography. These can be related to trade, investment hubs, oil and gas exploration sites on the High Seas and so on. Whenever a direct or indirect threat manifests to such interests, nation-states resolve to utilise the armed forces to secure them. Escorting of ships, naval patrols, and anti-piracy missions are some of the tasks that the Armed Forces carry out as part of securing the nation's economic interests, with 'Economic Diplomacy'.
- Nation-states conduct their inter-state relations through Coercive Diplomacy with the intent of achieving political objectives and fostering national interests without having to wage war. Threatening the adversary with possible consequences is unlike

conventional military strategy and is led by clear communication, signalling and bargaining to leave no doubt related to intentions and motives. The key variables in such actions are the balance of power in favour of the coercing state and the retention of control on the escalatory matrix. Military preparedness is thus vital for coercive diplomacy to be adopted by a nation-state.

- Another means that is adopted by nation-states, which rests heavily on the military preparedness of the state, is a 'show of force', which is a warning to an adversary, or a means to intimidate it, by displaying a capability. This can be carried out by carrying out test firing of weapons, training exercises close to the border or decapacitating the adversary's systems for a specific period.

Military preparedness will also be important in understanding how combat is evolving with the advancements in technologies and the emergence of new domains of warfare. The evolution of tactics to counter the envisaged methods of warfighting will also play an important role in deciding a nation's military preparedness. Force structures, duly supported by associated doctrines and concepts, will need to be created to give the Armed Forces the capability to respond to future threats through Multi-Domain Operations.

National Security Strategy

The original understanding of strategy was related to the military application of force. Largely it meant positioning of military forces to arrive at a favourable decision and, by application of military force, if the disposition itself does not lead to a favourable outcome. It was also referred to as 'Art of the General'. Strategy now has a wider understanding. It is the effective utilisation of resources to achieve the desired outcome and is used by companies, corporates, business houses and even universities. It links Ends and Means with Ways. Today, we can have a strategy for economic security, for development of education and infrastructure development. The private sector may have a strategy to overcome competition from peers and rivals.

No nation can secure itself without a strategy in place. The important constituents of a strategy would be Policy, Processes and Organisational Structures. I believe that India has all these functioning efficiently. India encountered the challenges of COVID-19 from zero preparation level to a nation acting in unison to propagating 'Vaccine Maitri'. It would not have been possible without all these being effective. Abrogation of Article 370 and bifurcation of the state of J&K into two union territories would not have been possible without all these elements that constitute the National Security Strategy and the basic security architecture being in place. Today, surgical strikes, multi-alignment, and Atmanirbharta are part of a strategy to secure the nation. It is possible because all organisational structures, processes and policies are in place. The resounding success of G-20 in the same manner promotes national interests, contributing to national security.

Strategic analysts and political pundits in India and abroad often have been found stating that India does not have a national security strategy. That is incorrect and a myopic understanding of the issue. What we don't have is a written document called the National Security Strategy, which is published periodically by some Western nations. Israel, the most threatened nation on earth, does not have a written policy document/ National Security Strategy. On the contrary, Pakistan issued a written National Security Policy in 2022 and soon ran into economic problems, political instability, rift between the Armed Forces and the citizens and problems on its western borders. They had the written document but lacked the organisational structures, processes and policies to secure the nation.

As we look towards the organisational structures responsible for national security in India, the National Security Council (NSC) is at the apex. Headed by the Honourable Prime Minister with the National Security Advisor (NSA) as a Secretary. It oversees both internal and external security about conventional and non-conventional threats, military affairs, space, cyber and technology. The National Security Council Secretariat (NSCS) functions under the aegis of the Prime

Minister Office (PMO) and is responsible for national security planning and coordination in the political, economic, energy and strategic arenas. It addresses current security threats, identifies emerging security challenges and then plans to build up capacities and resources to address these. It has three tiers.

The processes are steered through various committees like the Strategic Policy Group and Defence Planning Committee (DPC) which function under the chairmanship of the NSA. Other enabling committees include the Defence Acquisition Council which is headed by the Honourable Raksha Mantri and the Chiefs of Staff Committee to coordinate on the policy front for all tri-services military matters.

Conclusion

India aspires to be a developed nation on the centenary of its independence. National security, already complex will present a more complex mosaic in the future.

A conceptual framework of national security is essential for goal and role clarity among all those responsible for securing, defending and protecting the nation. There is also a requirement for military officers to understand the larger dynamics of national security without diluting the military preparedness aspect. The article only defines the conceptual framework of national security. The mosaic has to be filled with threats and challenges that we may face from our adversaries on the borders, in IOR, in space and in cyber domains. From the rising threat of terrorism and radicalisation on one end to the weaponisation of sanctions and the use of information as a weapon are major challenges that need to be dealt with.

Section B

WARFARE

5

The Nature of War and Types of Conflicts

"*War is an act of force to compel our enemy to do our will.*"

—Clausewitz

Introduction

Wars don't exist. Declared wars of the type we have witnessed in the history of modern warfare are obsolete. They do not exist anymore. Conflicts however exist. They are ubiquitous. We see them every day with increasing regularity on our TV screens and read about them in newspapers and on social/electronic media. While these statements open a set of debate, we cannot deny that warfare is becoming increasingly complex in today's era. It has made a wide set of thinkers review the entire conceptual landscape of war and warfare – from fundamental issues to its future conduct.

Conflicts arise due to the basic human nature of 'dominance' and 'self-preservation'. This relation of human nature with war has formed the basis of various theories on war. These theories have evolved from the times of Kingdoms to the times of the Westphalian State System and have established human nature as the main cause behind how organised kingdoms and states behave in times of war. These interrelations with humans have been based on various characteristics, be it 'fear, honour and interest' as contextualised by Thucydides or 'strong ruling over the weak being a just cause' as claimed by Thrasymachus.

These characteristics over some time have presented certain everlasting theories by great thinkers like Kautilya, Clausewitz, and Sun Tzu, who have propagated their thoughts on how war and warfare need to be viewed and conducted. While their thinking dimensions have continued to remain applicable in today's era, the bigger change which is emerging in recent times is the changing dimension of war itself.

At the larger geo-political level, war or combat has just become one end of a continuum. The adversarial actions between two actors have evolved into a continuum of Competition-Crisis-Confrontation-Conflict-Combat, which can be represented as 5Cs. Nations need not be in a single state at any time but more than one states may exist simultaneously even the opposing states may also co-exist. In this continuum, all elements of national power are used in varying degrees to achieve a favourable outcome. New intricacies are developing in these changing dimensions of war, guiding nations to demystify and visualise the shape and strategy for future wars. This visualisation requires reviewing the theoretical construct of war and warfare, including the basic nature of war and new dimensions of conflicts. This understanding is important as wars continue to shape the destiny of nations. After all no nation can conceive of entering war without understanding the nature of war, as the whole strategy to prosecute war depends upon it.

War, Violence and Its Elements

"Homo homini lupus est" a well-known Latin proverb which means "man is a wolf to man" is an apt way to express the violent nature of humans. The same nature of violence is equally applicable to clashes between established and organised states. This nature of resolution or domination where societal or political objectives escalate to a point of intense violence is termed as the point of war. Such intertwined relationships establish that war mainly comprises two parts: Violence and the Politics behind the violence.

The politics behind such violence have shaped certain defined dimensions of war over some time. These dimensions have framed the war as 'a just act' which is undertaken in a 'declared manner'. Such a framework has made people believe that war, when declared and executed even through extreme violence, is a justified action and a necessity for the self-preservation of the state and society.

The past wars from the ancient times through World Wars and even in today's era of Russia-Ukraine or Israel-Hamas conflicts, have made nations accept the unimaginable cost of war. But the real fact remains, that the cost of war is best measured by people who experience it. In a democratic society, the most peaceful people are the Generals. They understand the true cost of war. War may be spoken about and even eulogised by those who have no experience of it.

War and warfare have evolved from confrontation between primitive tribes, to battles between armed groups of agrarian societies, to Feudal Armies, to Armed Forces of Nation States to now multi-protagonist wars being fought in a globalised and interconnected world. To understand this evolution where the character and nature of war are getting reshaped, it is essential to first perceive what Combat or such levels of violence consist of. It mainly consists of four elements:

- Battle Space, where combat is executed. The arena where the contest takes place is strategically chosen for geographical and strategic advantages. It has a direct effect on who can participate in combat and how it has to be prosecuted. This space has today evolved from uni-dimensional to multi-dimensional.
- Combatant which includes soldiers to generals. In the current Westphalian model, the State has the only legal right to perpetuate violence. The state decides the justified reasons to declare war and execute violence to achieve politically defined objectives. This execution of violence is undertaken through the Armed Forces as the combatant and instrument of the State.
- Technology which manifests in the form of weapons, equipment and systems, impacts the processes for warfighting. As warfare evolves, technology has provided more and more options to execute combat. It has had a profound effect in revolutionising warfare and has made it more and more precise, lethal and far-

reaching. This rapid and continuous evolution has thereby changed the character of war. It has changed the landscape of how wars are fought. It is one of the main factors which have influenced the Tactics and Strategy utilised in the planning of combat.

- Strategy, that unfolds the positioning and movement of combatants interposed with technology. Every challenge to national security may require a definitive Military Strategy to overcome the odds and achieve success. Military Strategy to succeed must have the right blend of science and art. Strategy is engagement-centric and focused towards achieving the politico-military objectives of war.

These elements continue to remain interlinked and are fast changing. The battle space is continuously expanding with the emergence of new domains like space and cyber, necessitating the development of capabilities for multi-domain responses. Technology is ushering in the next Revolution of Military Affairs (RMA) cyclically thereby impacting methods of waging wars.

The combatant is now being seen as a protagonist coming in various shapes and forms, spanning from structured military organisations to non-structured, Para Military Forces (PMF). This is further complicated by the inclusion of mercenaries, contractors, jihadis and non-state actors, comprising both own as well as other state citizens.

New strategies are being evolved transforming traditional declared wars in many cases, to more informal and asymmetrical forms of warfare. This is a direct consequence of rapid geo-political changes and the VUCA environment where the World Order has given way to a Global Disorder. This disorder is visualised as durable with no legal acts being able to enforce peace. Confrontation and conflicts are assuming an enduring nature thereby even affecting how violence is being perpetuated. The emergence of such dimensions of combat or war is even influencing the 'Nature of War' and 'Types of Conflicts' envisaged in the future.

Nature of War: New Perspectives

There is a popular adage that the character of war is changing. It is always evolving primarily due to advancements in technology but the same adage also states that the basic nature of war has remained constant. The constant and unalterable nature of war finds its roots in Clausewitz and his two popular dictums enshrined in his seminal, yet unfinished work, 'On War'.

- The first is that war is organised violence for political ends. An alternate way to paraphrase it is by saying that war is a continuation of policy by other means.
- The second is that war is the imposition of one's will on the enemy. Violence is intrinsic to the imposition of will.

The above two postulates on the nature of war have remained unaltered along with an abstract conceptualisation of a larger understanding of what war is. In this abstract concept, war is normally associated with violence, death, destruction and cause of misery and suffering.

The question is, can political aims be achieved without recourse to war and the use of violence? While history has witnessed propounding numbers of deaths in various wars, there have been episodes where decisive results have also been achieved with no direct use of violence. It has guided strategists to evolve theories to support this approach.

- Sun Tzu's theoretic outlook on 'winning without fighting' can be best understood through a quote from his treatise, 'Art of War', "For to win one hundred victories in one hundred battles is not the acme of skill. To subdue the enemy without fighting is the acme of skill."
- Similarly, a British soldier, historian and theorist, Liddell Hart propagated through his work, Strategy: The Indirect Approach, had propagated that "The perfection of strategy would be to produce a decision without any serious fighting".

The focus of these theories has been towards adopting alternative methods to achieve victory before exercising the option of violence. The emphasis is on taking a set of decisive actions thereby creating a battle of dilemmas and fear, within the minds of the adversaries. Hence, the essence of Military Strategy as Liddell Hart states is, "Not so much to seek battle as to seek a strategic situation so advantageous that if it does not of itself produce the decision, its continuation by a battle is sure to achieve it".

The above two strategists focus on the movement and deployment of a military force to produce results and if that does not happen then going to the next level. However, today's context of warfare in the Cognitive domain exploits the basic human nature that no two individuals, even co-joined twins, can think alike. Every human mind being unique in itself can be influenced differently by well-crafted strategy.

Influence operations, perception management and the use of information as a weapon are enlarging conflict in the cognitive domain where public opinion is moulded to force a course of action by the government. The absence of physical violence that is generally associated with war is changing our visualisation of the very nature of war.

Similarly, the employment of economic sanctions or trade wars are inherently non-violent. Modern cyber operations further complicate the issue when state attribution can be denied, and the nature of the attack to be seen as war or not is more dependent on the attacked nation's perception than the attacker's intention. But the same is open to debate.

Types of Conflicts

Clausewitzian model for war is premised on the fact that going to war is more of a rational decision. While he conceptualises war with the trinity of emotion, chance and reason-based 'dominant tendencies', he also provides it with an institutionalised connection through a second trinity of people, army and government. This relation attempts to present war as a formal act which is executed post-rational deliberation.

This thought has also been based on the visualisation of a primordial nature of violence as a means to achieve political ends. It may now be changing with violence being undertaken in many cases for the sake of violence. It is no longer a means but has attained the end state itself. This has resulted in the rationality in some of the physical wars being fought today being absent. One of the best examples of such wars or warfare is Jihad and Terrorism.

In Terrorism one finds the absence of a political goal. It is not a means to an end but an end in itself. In the Quranic concept of war, terror is not a means to impose a decision but a decision in itself. Such violence without any definite political end state is contributing to the changing nature of war. In another dimension, it has been brought to the fore that war is no more a clash only between the armed forces of two organised states but can be through the inclusion of non-organised participants also.

The presence of non-state actors, perpetrating an undeclared format of war with an unending context has introduced the lexicon of 'Informal Wars'. The relevance of such wars has only increased with time due to the long absence of formal wars. However, the term 'Informal War' has introduced a casualness in the very serious business of war. War even in a sub-conventional format retains its serious character.

The participation of such non-state belligerents has made Hybrid and Asymmetric Warfare become an essential part of every modern conflict. Recent conflicts like Russia and Ukraine have proven that power asymmetry and the hybrid conduct of warfare can be achieved through the combined usage of traditional state forces and such contracted non-state forces.

Such asymmetric conduct of the war has further formalised the pre-Cold War-era concept of 4th Generation warfare, wherein the lines between war and policy get blurred. This asymmetry is not being achieved only in the kinetic dimension but has even found relevance in forms of non-kinetic action in the war of 'information and perception' or 5th Generation Warfare.

This non-traditional, asymmetric and new-generation warfare has made externally supported non-state actor employment a reality. This proxy war which India has been subjected to for decades is now witnessing more awareness. Israel-Hamas conflict is a classical example where the concomitant application of Hezbollah and Houthis is presenting a complex face of future warfare.

The near permanence and enduring nature of conflict have been closely witnessed in recent decades. A testimony to this can be established through the occurrence of multiple Insurgency and Low-Intensity Conflicts all around the world. It should therefore be widely accepted that conflict as a continuum has become a perpetual activity. This era has become an era of Sub-Conventional Warfare where peaceful co-existence is a distant dream and simmering fears of war nearly a certainty, especially in certain geographies that have a history of disputes.

Measuring victory in the complex and ambiguous conduct of war was always a difficult task. However, the mere nature of permanence in these armed conflicts below the threshold of classical war has made defining matrices of victory in sub-conventional war a huge challenge. This method of war has a series of other challenges that are required to be addressed to ensure that if not victory but at least the intent is achieved and demonstrated.

Challenges of Sub-Conventional War

Sudden acts of terror will attract a lower threshold of tolerance from the adversary. This was evident in Uri and Balakot and on a larger scale, in Gaza. Such a response needs the intrinsic involvement of many instruments of national power due to the increased risk of escalation. It requires a stage-managed execution where every possible response by the adversary has to be thought of and balanced effectively to achieve escalation dominance.

Sub-conventional ops are based on two critical elements – a short time of response and a well-synchronised plan. To achieve these critical requirements, a higher readiness level is required. This requires a perpetual need for alertness by the entire security apparatus of the nation.

The complexity of such operations reduces dependencies on violence-based options. These options are capable of sending a strategic signal which is precise and impactful and sometimes is even found as the most suitable option. This has mainly happened due to the emergence of a wide set of options through the domains of Cyber, and Space. These options are equally potent to achieve the desired intent while receiving the threshold of violence.

The ability to apply violence within specific limits while retaining control over the escalation matrix is even being seen in traditional domains. For example, the older mindset that every action through the medium of air will be escalatory in nature is changing. The applicability of such measured options is now being seen in increased occasions. Whether it was PLAAF manoeuvres in the Taiwan strait, United States Air Force (USAF) kinetic actions against Chinese surveillance balloons, Israeli air strikes in Syria and Lebanon, Russian air activities near NATO airspace, and even recent offensive exchanges in our neighbourhood between Iran and Pakistan are some examples where duels in air domain have not led to uncontrolled escalation.

The efficacy of intertwined execution and perception management has brought media and information management to war rooms. Information warfare has a dynamic and ever-alive character, especially in controlling specific actions in a sub-conventional environment. It has resulted in the information warrior being deployed from media centres or hacking sites to front lines, to carry out every action in time to outmanoeuvre the adversary. This dynamic stage management involves the fine balancing of actions between various elements of the state and has an associated set of challenges. The demands of this non-linear approach towards operations have started affecting conventional strategy and are also envisaged to even impact future designs of force structures.

Grey Zone Warfare

These new dimensions of warfare are now being presented under a new lexicon of Grey Zone Warfare which aims to exploit the operational space between peace and war. It is described as a well-crafted military action carried out below the threshold of inviting a conventional military response. The dividend of such a strategy emerges after a long gestation period. It is different from a Western construct of warfighting which focuses on the 'Decisive Military Action'. In Grey Zone, the focus is on 'Timely Military Action'.

In such a warfare political ends are planned to be achieved without recourse to violence which somewhat puts a question mark on Clausewitz's dictum on the nature of war. Grey Zone warfare hence lies in the opposite spectrum of terrorism, where the focus is on violence without any political end state. Here again, there is the absence of physical violence that is generally associated with the abstract conceptualisation of war that may change how we visualise the nature of war.

Future Wars

While a theoretical construct of war and warfare attempts to generalise the subject, it is to be accepted that every war is unique in itself. This eternal truth will find its applicability even in future wars, despite its changing nature and the emergence of new methods of warfare.

This uniqueness is brought in due to a large number of differing factors. Every state has its own set of political objectives guiding the development of its policy towards any future war. Every battle space is different due to its geography and varied combination of domains.

The protagonist of every war is different, in future, we might even see robots and humanoids as combatants. The capability of every force will be different due to differing technological thresholds. And most important, to execute every future war, even the Strategy for every war will be required to be different. The end point is that the nature of war is changing. Earlier it was believed that only the character of war changes. Hence, we must be prepared politically and militarily to face challenges emerging out of the changing nature of war.

This chapter has attempted to uncover the sheaths of a complex and smeared cover of war and its future contour. While contemporary thoughts will find their relevance even in today's era, it is these new indications which need acceptance. Such an attempt will ensure that while we aim to be future-ready for any eventuality, our efforts are aimed in the correct direction.

6

Evolving Battlefield Architecture

"The modernday battlespace has exploded not only in terms of the domains but also in terms of the players that inhabit each domain."

—Author

War and Warfare

Domination and self-preservation are basic human instincts that lead to violence. When these instincts are unchecked or manipulated, they can lead to conflicts and aggression. In organised societies, these instincts may manifest on a larger scale, where power struggles between groups may escalate into violent confrontations. If perpetuated in a planned manner, such acts may be called war. Wars, throughout history, have often reflected these primal instincts where nations vie for dominance, territory or resources, driven by a collective urge for self-preservation and the desire to assert control over others.

War and Warfare are as old as human civilisation and soldiering is one of the oldest professions. Throughout the ages, soldiers have been revered as protectors, defenders and enforcers of a state's authority. While motivations for war and the methods of soldiering have varied across cultures and periods, the fundamental role of soldiers in defending interests, maintaining order and asserting power remains constant.

Impact of Technology on Warfare

Warfare has evolved from confrontation between primitive tribes when man was still a hunter-gatherer, to conflicts between feudal armies of an agrarian society to armed forces of nation-states in the industrialised world to now multi-protagonist wars being fought in a globalised and interconnected world. War and Conflict may be confrontations between organised forces in the field or between unorganised groups but its outcome has always been influenced by superior technology and accompanying tactics.

An ancient or medieval infantryman relied on a short sword, helmet and body armour. The lance and pike introduced concepts of infantry formations. The longbow and crossbow added targeting at longer ranges. The introduction of the stirrup revolutionised cavalry tactics, allowing for greater stability and effectiveness in mounted combat. The discovery of gunpowder heralded a new era of warfare enabling the creation of cannons and firearms that could breach fortifications and pierce armour, deciding the outcome of many battles. Subsequent innovations and the introduction of technologies like tanks, aircraft and missiles further transformed the tactics and strategies employed in modern warfare, leading to new doctrines and approaches to combat.

Battlefield, Battle Space and Staff

Until the middle of the 19th century, warfare primarily unfolded on a single battlefield. Armies would converge on a designated battlefield, often chosen strategically for its geographical advantages, wherein, the combatants would engage and the outcome segregated the victor and the vanquished. Battles from Kurukshetra to Kalinga, Plassey to Panipat in India and those in the Western world like Marathon, Austerlitz, Jena and Waterloo to Tours were all fought on a single battlefield. Command and Control of such battles were easier and the outcome was decided in a matter of days if not hours.

In the middle of the 19th Century, two unexpected technologies, not related to warfighting, profoundly influenced the character of warfare. These were the advent of Railways and the invention of the Telegraph. The former could transport armies to geographically displaced areas, and mobilise cavalry, artillery and logistics to support battles at different locations. The latter revolutionised warfare as geographically displaced armies could now be controlled from a distance. Flags, flares, smoke, messengers and ADC of yore were replaced by the telegraph line which followed the advancing armies. These two inventions enabled wars to be fought on distant battlefields. It introduced the concept of 'fronts', a precursor to 'Theatres' and expanded the battle space in terms of both 'Time and Space'.

The temporal and spatial expansion of the battlefield gave birth to an important link between the leader and the led, between the commander and his troops – the General Staff. On a single battlefield, usually the sovereign or on his behalf, a commander would coordinate the deployment, movement and application of forces. His reading of the battle, based on experience and gut instincts generally decided the outcome. Most of the time, his orders were communicated directly to the subordinate commander leading fighting formations or reserve echelons.

The French can be credited with starting the concept of 'Staff' by raising the Quartermaster General Staff. This staff, as the name suggested, was required for the billeting of troops. The Germans, however, refined this concept by introducing formal training for their 'General Staff'. The General Staff was responsible for the continuous study of all aspects of war and for drawing up and reviewing plans for mobilisation or conduct of a campaign. The General Staff was first established by law in Germany in 1814. Gradually, Quartermaster and Adjutant General Staff functioning evolved separately from Operations and Intelligence.

This concept provided major dividends during the Franco-Prussian war in 1870–1871, wherein, the German Army could achieve greater success primarily because of the application of better administration, planning and professional knowledge by the formally trained General Staff. Prussian and German military victories towards the end of the 19th Century can be credited to their professionalism as well as the Command Leadership. Handling field operations was important, but effective staff work was also starting to be seen as critical to the success of operations. The concept of Chief of Staff operating under the Commander in Chief was adopted by most European armies by the turn of the 19th Century. A support structure in the form of a General HQ and Regional/ Theatre HQs to control the war effort also started taking shape.

Expansion of Battle Space

Warfare gradually entered the maritime domain when wind-powered coastal ships graduated to ocean-going cruisers and destroyers powered by steam and later by fossil fuels. Military power could now be exercised over distant lands, especially over those nations which did not have this capability. The advent of the air force brought a new dimension and domain in modern warfare. In wars, the outcome was now increasingly being decided in the new domain, especially in the opening stages of conflict with capabilities of older domains coming into play later.

WW-I and WW-II expanded the battlefield over land, maritime and aerial domains to be called battle space. The new battle space was not only more dispersed, it contained elements of three services. Marines and Airborne forces bridged the gap between sea-land warfare at one end and land-aerial warfare at the other. The geo-politics of great wars produced allies and adversaries. The battlefield was now populated by multi-national forces operating in the tri-services domain. This produced its challenges for the Commander as well as the Staff.

Explosion of Battle Space

Traditionally, warfare has been confined to physical domains such as land, sea and air. However, today the complexity of warfare has increased manifold as wars not only can be fought simultaneously in these physical domains but are also affected by the emergence of new domains such as cyber, space, underwater and the electromagnetic spectrum.

- ***Cyber Space.*** Cyber is a manmade domain. It is for this reason that Cyber Space cannot be considered neutral. The traditional domains of warfare, save for the technological edge, provide a level playing field to the belligerents. This is not true for Cyber Space as it can be controlled and manipulated.

- ***Space.*** In traditional domains, the belligerents fought and survived in that domain. They could directly influence operations. However, currently, all operations in space are being controlled through the surface domain. Technology is yet to evolve to put combatants in space to decide the outcome. However, the control of territory on celestial bodies like the moon may become a matter of competition, contest and conflict in the future and emerge as a separate domain.
- ***Underwater.*** The ubiquity and omnipresence of sensors and the ability to target what can be detected will push maritime operations into the underwater domain. Sea bed resources are another factor for underwater dominance in the future. The control of forces in the underwater domain and combat situations will tax the future Commanders as well as Staff.
- ***Electro-Magnetic (EM) Spectrum.*** Like Space, this too is a domain where combatants cannot reside to fight. It is an enabler which has to be controlled to gain Combat Superiority.

The synthetic and man-made domains of Cyber and EM Spectrum are ever-expanding. In such emerging domains, and to some extent even Space, there is little difference between staff and combatants/combat units. Both their functions merge as control over such battle space is being exercised from outside. Another aspect is the non-kinetic nature of actions that don't put the life of combat elements (or staff) at risk and danger, yet the consequences of actions could be catastrophic on systems that help manage the economy, public services and even kinetic operations of war. It adds a new dimension, physical and psychological, to modern warfare.

Cyber and EM Spectrum could also be considered as environments through which one has to operate. Such an environment poses risk and danger at every moment of peace and war. It is like CBRN which must be considered as an environment in which one has to live, survive and if required fight through, rather than considering it as a threat. In such an environment, every element of the war machinery has to take protective measures. The role of Commanders and staff in such an environment becomes more complex and demanding.

New types of soldiers have also contributed to the explosion of battle space. Combatants today include organised Armed Forces, non-state actors such as terrorists, mercenaries, contractors, civilians, citizens of other nations and as observed in the case of Ukraine, even students and amateurs. The wars of the future may feature Robots as a part of the combat force. Unmanned and autonomous weapons are already part of the modern battlefield. Warfare in multiple domains has therefore emerged as a pervasive and enduring threat. The battlespace today has 'No Fronts, No Flanks and No Rear'. It has become a concept of 'ultimate non-linearity'. Threats can now emanate from any possible direction at any place and at any time.

Cognitive Domain

In today's VUCA world, we face the prospect of geo-political aims being achieved without recourse to violence at all. Warfare in the cognitive domain is being increasingly used to mould public opinions to seek a favourable geo-political outcome. This in some manner questions the abstract understanding of the nature of war where 'violence and destruction' are associated with imposing one's own will on the enemy. The battle space has expanded into the cognitive domain, wherein, decision-making processes are shaped by leveraging various means such as propaganda, psychological operations and strategic communication. These tactics in the cognitive domain are being increasingly utilised to manipulate perceptions, sow the seeds of confusion and gain strategic advantages.

Artificial Intelligence aided deep fakes, digital twins and fake news are emerging as critical psychological warfare tools. They can be employed for spreading disinformation and deception. By the size of the audience that they influence, they are a significant threat to National Security. Influencing public opinion by obscuring the truth or creating customised truths, thus can cause chaos, and confusion and create uncertainties around military operations. Deep fake experimentation and execution have been highly visible in the ongoing Russia-Ukraine war.

Amidst this changing geo-political landscape, it is difficult to predict the trajectory of future warfare with accuracy, as it does not follow a linear progression at times due to the convergence of disruptive technologies. The methodology of conducting war is evolving at an equally fast pace, mandating new concepts and doctrinal transformation. Staff analysis is being replaced by computation, algorithms, and software/applications. Real-time Battle Field Transparency through Data-Centric Architecture, Swifter Decision Making, and Joint Theatre of Operations are increasingly becoming mandatory for battle readiness and the attainment of military objectives.

The changing paradigm of warfighting and the propensity of nation-states to adopt violent means for conflict termination have exponentially increased the variables for forecasting and preparing for future wars. Military commanders are continually adapting to keep pace in a multitude of domains with their potential adversaries, both known and unknown. Synchronisation and orchestration of all instruments available for the application of force are fundamental to contemporary warfighting. Such an approach is all the more necessary in a resource-constrained environment where maximising the efficiency of converting 'Capital' to 'Combat Power' is a key determinant of the outcome of conflict.

Conclusion

The modern-day battlespace has exploded not only in terms of the domains but also in terms of the players that inhabit each domain. Land, Air, Maritime including underwater, Cyber, Space, EM Spectrum, and Cognitive comprise both state and non-state actors, making warfare a very complex business. And it hasn't peaked yet – it continues to evolve and become more complex even today. The state of flux that the World Geo-politics is in today makes the future very uncertain. Preparing for this uncertain future in terms of threats and vulnerabilities is the biggest challenge that we face today. The type of conflict that we may be subjected to in times to come remains opaque with an occasional window of transparency.

To prepare for these tumultuous and uncertain times, in the emerging complex battlespace, Commanders and Staff need to work in close cohesion as one team. Battlefield decisions, owing to the diverse and variegated nature of the battlespace, will continue to be more demanding and complicated.

The focus on operations will be demanding as an outcome of the above factors and hence will need considerable time and thought. Operational inputs therefore will need to be segregated from administrative and other inputs. Force employment will per-force have to be separated from Force development and Force sustenance, despite their intricate linkages. Technological advancements have made the seemingly fictitious Hyper Wars, where algorithms control warfare, a near reality. In such a scenario, the Commander and staff will need to exercise more human control in decision-making.

7

Tactics Led Force Modernisation

> *"Knowledge gives you the ability to look at an issue from different perspective and from an unconditional domain. One will have to be innovative, inventive, indigenous and imaginative to impose our will on the enemy."*
>
> —Author

Introduction

Force Modernisation aims primarily to keep pace with emerging technologies, bridge the gap and hence significantly enhance capabilities to meet contemporary and future challenges. It involves not only modernising equipment but also modernising doctrinal concepts, tactics, techniques and procedures. This span of modernisation is challenged by the evolving and dynamic nature of the security environment around us. The dynamism and ever-expanding dimension of battle space have led decision-makers, developers and practitioners to understand the uniqueness of combat, which would provide the right framework for conceptualising future force modernisation.

Uniqueness of Combat

Clausewitz in 'On War' has rightly said, that 'Every age has its kind of war, its limiting conditions, and its peculiar preconceptions'. Every war is unique. It is because it takes place in a unique geo-political setting. The politico-military objective of any war India faces must be unique to us. Hence, the strategy that flows from it for the attainment of politico-military objectives will be unique. The possibility of such a strategy succeeding will be higher if the tactics and technology that support the strategy are indigenous.

Developing an Indian strategy will require an in-depth analysis of the intricacies which are specific to India, based on her historical episodes, adversarial situation and geographical position. These intricacies present a unique set of combat scenarios for India and can be visualised in five ways.

The first uniqueness is the diversity of domains in which combat will be conducted both due to our geographical location as well as possible adversarial situations. Our nation with a large landmass of mainland as well as island territories, has a wide variety of terrain spreading from plains, mountains, and deserts to dense forest areas. It presents a unique set of complexity in the land domain. Similarly, our large coastline, Exclusive Economic Zone (EEZ), wide ocean areas and central location in the Indian Ocean Region (IOR) presents its own set of uniqueness in the maritime domain. The wide volumes of airspaces above our land and maritime territories which are becoming denser with manned and unmanned platforms present a unique set of complexities in the air domain as well. In addition to these conventional domains, the new domains of cyber, space and information also present a diverse set of challenges that are required to be addressed.

The second set of uniqueness is the type of players who are operating in these domains. They include not only State but Non-State actors as well. They are not only restricted to uniformed forces but also include State-sponsored terrorists and militia who not only operate around our external boundaries but also within our Nation. This internal threat dimension is further cluttered due to the presence of insurgents. The introduction of invisible players like cyber and information warriors has further complicated the situation.

The next uniqueness is the types of conflict which we as a nation face in the continuum of Peace, No War No Peace to War. It is not only classical dimensions of War but the zone of No War No Peace where we are witnessing a wide set of conflicts. In this part of the continuum, insurgency and terrorism are presenting new dimensions of conflicts through the emergence of piracy and cross-border drone strikes-based threats. As we progress ahead on this continuum, Low-Intensity Conflict in localised zones has become the norm with a realistic possibility of graduating into a classical war. Our Armed Forces need to be ready for the entire span of conflicts.

The next uniqueness is that targeting is not only restricted to physical damage but is now being equally focused towards the Cognitive dimension. Seamless and quick information flow has created a transparent environment which can be easily influenced. It has resulted in every citizen becoming a possible target creating a surge in several vulnerabilities.

The last uniqueness is a ramification of all of the above-mentioned unique factors. To address the requirements of these factors mentioned earlier, specific capabilities and capacities are required to be developed. The identification of the correct balance between all these factors would require a stipulation of the level and depth of capabilities, which need to be augmented. It requires creating the ideal mix of capabilities within the domain-specific Services and various combatants and support mechanisms within every Service. The achievement of such an ideal mix requires understanding the key aspects which necessitate force modernisation.

Key Factors Behind Force Modernisation

Modernisation of the military is a necessity for every nation. The complex set of factors that influence modernisation are more or less common to all the militaries across the world.

The first is the environment in and around the country. It plays a primary role in deciding the security needs of the Nation. The second factor is the capability threshold of the military for maintaining an asymmetric advantage over the adversaries. The technological threshold within the nation, both in terms of production as well as innovation, is the next factor, which plays an important role in forcing modernisation. Budget and policy on force modernisation in the nation is the next factor which defines the pace and extent of modernisation as well. The complexity of these factors needs to be balanced by defining a path towards modernisation, a path which is either technology-driven or tactics-driven.

The Primacy of Tactics or Technology

It is generally believed that Technology has had a major influence on the conduct of combat. Technology is the focal arbitrator that tilts the balance between equally motivated adversaries. On the other hand, it can be argued that necessity is the mother of invention. A felt need during combat may lead to the development of a particular weapon system.

Unlike a 'Chicken and Egg' story, in today's world, most of the technologies are dual use. Military technology finds application in the civilian domain and vice versa. GPS, Internet, and SDR were primarily developed for the military and have widespread civil applications today. LIDAR, Drones, and Satellites were for civilian use but have military applications. One has to have a keen eye for selecting and adopting technology. This guides nations to adopt either a technology-led or tactics-led approach towards modernisation when it comes to developing capacities for the warfighting.

Technology Led Modernisation

In a 'Technology Led Force Modernisation' approach, new technological options emerge and mature with time. These new technologies are adopted by militaries wherein new concepts are developed and existing Tactics, Techniques and Procedures (TTPs) are reviewed. A training mechanism is later followed to ensure that new methods of force employment are completely adopted by the entire organisation.

In India, we have been pursuing Technology-led modernisation till now. The Services identify a key weapon system/technology that is required for induction. The GSQRs of such a platform are laid and DRDO is tasked to acquire the capability, mostly through a Mission Mode project. The system, if it meets the QRs, its prototypes are trial evaluated and on its clearance, the technology is shared with a DPSU (or now a private entity) for mass production. In a modification to this process, DRDO may choose a private entity under the DCPP model for co-development and co-production. The larger point is that our system of modernisation/acquisition of a capability is based on a weapon system/platform/technology that already exists. It not only takes years to develop it but another few years for Services to assimilate it into existing systems or raise new ones. In this system, we will always be behind the curve concerning modern militaries.

Tactics Led Modernisation

In a 'Tactics Led Modernisation' approach, the combatants lead the process of modernisation. The fighting arms decide the type of combat they will be faced with or how they wish to employ force against the adversary. In this approach, a core team identifies the range of technologies that will support that concept of warfighting. Some of these technologies may exist, may need modification/adaptation or some may have to be developed anew. To execute this approach, the team is funded for the realisation of the project. It may outsource R&D or modification of technology to academicians, IITs, tech incubators, and military or civil R&D establishments.

The model may require three to four service teams working on the realisation of a new concept. Ideally, it would demand setting up an integrated team of strategists, tacticians and developers, who can develop key concepts which are peculiar to their conditions and terrain and would assist in the achievement of an asymmetric advantage over the adversary. The technological developments emerging from tactical (warfighting) concepts being country-specific will remain effective in terms of absorption, employment and further re-adaptation.

The concept of building a Smart Battalion can be taken as an example to understand this approach. A Smart Battalion focuses on the intelligent way of warfighting. A Special Forces battalion focuses on kinetic engagements at operational level, whereas a Smart Battalion will focus on intelligent engagements with disproportionate effects at operational or strategic level. The technological threshold of our soldiers is low. It will take ages to improve their technological threshold to fight smart. Whereas, the Smart Battalion is a set of technologically oriented men who are distributed across the large battle zone. 40 to 50 of such entities comprising of 2 to 3 smart soldiers each, could be spread in the battle space thus being undetectable and untargetable. They would control surveillance, target acquisition and targeting, like a mobile and dispersed Corps/Division Intelligence and Surveillance Centre (CISC/DISC).

To implement this concept, certain special technologies would be required to be inducted or developed. These might include technologies like secure long-range communication, plug-and-play systems, sensor fusion set-up, mobile decision support systems, and adaptable survival kits to name a few. Such an approach would have dual benefits in terms of both streamlining force modernisation efforts as well as achieving an asymmetrical edge over the adversary.

India's Force Modernisation Approach: A Choice to Make

As a Nation, we have a choice to make. We need to choose whether we would follow a 'Technology Led' or 'Tactics Led' force modernisation. With the technological development edge being with major powers, we as a nation are forced to adopt a follower approach wherein, we end up waiting for new technologies to crystallise and later are forced to chase the process of technological absorption, tactics development and even organisational re-orientation in an unplanned manner. It results in always being behind the curve. To remain ahead of the curve Atmanirbharta initiative has provided our nation with a possible solution. A 'Tactics Led' approach would not only assure that we develop an asymmetric edge over our adversaries through indigenous solutions but also achieve the aim of setting up a self-reliant world-class defence ecosystem in our nation. It would ensure that we can enter the era of modern war along with the West, breaking the shackles of being a follower.

It is indeed tragic that India, which was a pioneer in ancient times, introducing the world to pivotal concepts like zero, medical breakthroughs and astrology, has been forced to follow advanced nations in technological breakthroughs. In the military and national security domain, there is a need for an intellectual transformation alongside technological absorption. It has to be followed by changes in organisation, culture, mindset and behaviour. It would require a holistic and realistic visualisation of future warfighting wherein an optimum balance between the old and new options is conceived.

Modalities to be Adopted: 'Tactics Led' Force Modernisation

The key to success in the 'Tactics Led' force modernisation would depend on the effective adoption of an integrated approach – both between the Services as well as between the Civil and Military agencies. These integrated teams would have to plan for various modalities while adopting this approach. The first step would be an integrated threat assessment with the intent to identify the key tactics which can be developed to achieve asymmetry against the adversaries. It would require utilising a re-modelled set up of tacticians, op planners, strategists, testers and developers. These novel tactics would provide the base for the next step of developing futuristic concepts and identifying specific technological requirements that will be required to prosecute developed concepts.

An imaginative fighting methodology would require the support of an analytical framework for finding realistic solutions and shortening the path from ideation to implementation. It will involve identifying whether the technological requirements can be met within the nation or would require international collaboration – based on Technology Readiness Level (TRL) and Manufacturing Readiness Level (MRL). This would provide the framework of rank ordering technological gestation period vis-à-vis prioritisation of tactical gaps.

The complexity at this stage would demand the utilisation of simulation-based war game mechanisms to identify the impact of identified capabilities in various scenarios. The employment of each technological capability in a stimulatory mechanism will provide the initial guidelines for the development of a prototype.

The prototype would then be fielded in specific exercises and war games involving both Red and Blue forces to test its efficacy in actual conditions. The feedback received through this action would be utilised for undertaking further enhancements/modifications in the prototype. It would also provide clarity in the development of doctrinal concepts. The base concept and efficacy of the prototype in operations would be shared with the Services for induction-related deliberations and planning.

Conclusion

'Multi-domain operations (MDO)' have become inevitable, flexible and sophisticated wherein response options have to be optimum for the entire conflict continuum. These response options if based on non-indigenous concepts would always carry the danger of being non-effective in our battle zones. In addition to indigenous concepts, there would also be a requirement to adopt not only indigenous equipment but an indigenous network architecture as well.

The necessity of such an architecture in present times can be seen when Network Centric Warfare (NCW) or Data Centric Warfare (DCW) have become the backbone for the conduct of operations. Such an NCW or DCW set-up is based on platforms and sensors supported by a complex network of computers, sensors, and terrestrial and satellite links. The combat management system architecture for such a set-up would have to be indigenous. In addition, this architecture should also have the ability to integrate non-indigenous platforms based on operational necessity. Setting up such an architecture would ensure that the capabilities of our future battle systems evolve and expand in sync with operational necessities.

To develop such a robust mechanism, we as a nation and military will have to embrace a far-sighted approach towards force modernisation following the path of imagination and innovative thinking. Our ancient wisdom will have to be used as a source of inspiration. It will inspire all of us, that we were leaders once and can become once again. This intent would require belief in our capabilities and strength. As mentioned in Rig Veda, 'Aano Bhadra Kartvo Yantu Vishwatah', we would also have to welcome good ideas and develop them with full support and zeal.

India is at the cusp of great change and correct actions at this stage are necessary to build the core of technological strength within the nation. We have laid down our path to become a 'Viksit and Sashakt Bharat'. It is, therefore of prime importance that the intellectual control and direction of what technologies are required needs to be firmly entrenched within the Armed Forces, with assistance from academia, DPSUs, DRDO and technocrats. A correct approach by the defence ecosystem during these times will ensure that we can transform our thoughts, skills and capabilities that are essential for building a 'Future Ready Armed Force'.

8

Preparing for the Third Revolution in Military Affairs

> "*India must prepare itself for the third revolution in military affairs, which is driven by technological advancements and the need for rapid adaptation to new types of conflicts.*"
>
> —NSA Ajit Doval

Introduction

One of the most enduring aspects of human civilisation is its propensity towards organised violence. Known by various terms like battle, war and conflict, the foundational aim of such an activity has always remained the same: use calibrated violence to achieve a political goal. The way wars are being fought, however, has undergone a fundamental change over the last few hundred years. Foremost among the causal factors are technological changes restructuring of state-society relations and productivity improvement. Combined with doctrinal evolution and adaptation within organisational structures, these produce what are known as Revolutions in Military Affairs (RMA).

Brief History of RMA

RMA may be defined as a "discontinuous increase in military capability and effectiveness". It occurs when technology is introduced in large numbers and is accompanied by changes in tactics, followed by changes in organisational structure that supports the tactics and technology. The introduction of the term RMA can be credited to the Department of Defence of the US, especially the Office of Net Assessment (ONA).

However, the initial concerns about rapid advancements in technology, especially related to non-nuclear weapon systems by Soviet analysts, resulted in the introduction of the term Military Technical Revolution (MTR). While MTR was concerned solely with the impact of (then) emerging technologies on warfare, RMA was holistic as it tried to look back into history and analyse the turning points where technological changes combined with operational innovations and organisational adaptations in military systems could dramatically improve military effectiveness and fundamentally alter the character and conduct of military operations. When it comes to the contemporary era, two perceptible RMAs have changed the concepts of modern wars.

The First RMA

The first RMA was the 'Maneuver Warfare' which occurred due to advances in surface and air mobility, along with long-range weapons that included Tanks, ICVs, Self-propelled Guns and Helicopters. It made the simultaneity and synchronisation of the Air-Land battle and Deep Battles possible. The foundation of manoeuvre warfare can be traced back to the principles and tactics of the German 'Blitzkrieg' employed during World War II. Blitzkrieg translates to a 'lightning war' and emphasises the use of rapid movement, surprise and coordinated attacks to disrupt enemy lines and achieve decisive victories. Instead of engaging in prolonged battles of attrition, it focused on exploiting weaknesses in enemy defences, bypassing strong points and encircling enemy forces to quickly achieve strategic objectives. The essence of agility and surprise that characterised 'Maneuver Warfare' introduced tactical concepts such as Envelopment, Turning Movement, Penetration and Tempo, Operational Fires and Shaping of the Battlefield at the operational level. The 'First RMA' also brought in several technical concepts such as the Centre of Gravity, Culmination Point, Projection Areas, Simultaneity, Synchronisation and Non-linearity.

The Second RMA

Similarly, 'Net-Centric Warfare (NCW)' was the second RMA that happened due to technological advancement in Information and

Communications Technologies (ICT) and computation power. It brought in concepts like Battle Field Transparency (BFT), Situational Awareness and Spectrum Domination. The foundation of NCW was laid in the Kosovo War and the Gulf War as its tenets were effectively utilised enabling better situational awareness, faster decision-making and more agile responses to changing battlefield conditions.

The availability of real-time Intelligence, Surveillance and Reconnaissance inputs through satellite imagery, unmanned aerial vehicles (UAVs) and reconnaissance aircraft coupled with their rapid dissemination ensured Situational Awareness. The integration of Command, Control, Communication, Computers and Intelligence (C4I) enabled the exchange of information. These together facilitated swifter decision-making. The use of Precision Guided Munitions (PGMs) was enabled by network centricity thus enhancing operational efficacy. The 'interconnectivity' between military forces, secure communication networks and shared databases added to operational efficiency in terms of interoperability and integration.

These wars established NCW as a Force Multiplier which can maximise the combat potential of military forces by integrating various assets like sensors, platforms and weapons systems, thereby enhancing the synergy and coordination between different elements. This ushered in the second RMA, wherein, advanced militaries realised the huge scope of its applicability across all tenets of modern war, particularly its ability to enable military forces to respond rapidly to changing battlefield conditions and emerging threats. The Indian Armed Forces have also upgraded their NCW capabilities for the conduct of Multi-Domain Operations in a Net-Centric environment through systems like the Integrated Air Command and Control System (IACCS) of the Indian Air Force, Indian Maritime Situational Awareness System (IMSAS) of the Indian Navy and Battlefield Surveillance System (BSS) of the Indian Army.

The International Fusion Centre – IOR (IFC-IOR) at Gurugram with its robust net-centric architecture has been playing a crucial role in fostering cooperation, coordination and collaboration among regional and international navies and maritime agencies to address common maritime security challenges effectively. Similarly, for the Army, the Division Information and Surveillance Centre (DISC) and the Corps Information and Surveillance Centre (CISC) are critical components of the Indian Army's intelligence and surveillance infrastructure, that are emerging as important elements in providing actionable intelligence to support military operations at the divisional and corps levels. These improvements in NCW capability have resulted in shifting of the control of operations to higher levels like Air Warfare has transited to 'Centralised Planning and Decentralised Execution' with operations being monitored and controlled from the Command level.

The Third RMA

The world is on the cusp of a Third RMA. This new threshold is developing due to rapid technological innovations in the fields of Robotics, Machine Learning (ML), Big Data Analysis, Artificial intelligence, Hypersonic and Quantum. It is difficult to presently define the exact shape and contours of such an RMA. It is important, however, to understand that the newer generation of RMA does not make the older generations obsolete. The concurrent events in various domains, types of conflicts and new methods of warfare are still evolving and progressively increasing the levels of complexity.

Some predict that we will move from Net Centric to Data Centric Warfare where Data Analytics, Artificial Intelligence (AI) and ML will play a major role. Others say that the battlespace will become more automated, autonomous and non-contact-based. The increasing capabilities of Information and Non-Contact Warfare are having a significant impact on how warfare is being viewed, thought and executed. We are witnessing a change not only in the 'character' but also in the 'nature' of war. The complexities of the 3rd RMA can be grouped under one term as 'Convergence Warfare' which I believe will essentially have three components – Data Centric Warfare, Celerity Centric Warfare and Info-Centric Warfare.

Data-Centric Warfare

Data is the new oil. In the future, data will play a central role in shaping the global economy, driving advancements in technology, industry, commerce and military. Organisations that can effectively collect, analyse and leverage data will gain a competitive edge, driving productivity, efficiency and innovation across sectors. The availability of relevant data significantly influences the conduct of Modern Warfare. Military operations increasingly rely on data-driven approaches, leveraging information technology, sensors and data analytics to enhance situational awareness, decision-making and operational effectiveness. Data is used to gather intelligence, conduct predictive analysis and support precision targeting, enabling military forces to achieve their objectives with greater precision and efficiency.

Artificial Intelligence (AI), Machine Learning (ML), computing power and the development of complex algorithms are key drivers for the transition to Data-Centric Warfare (DCW). These together enable military forces to process and analyse vast amounts of data quickly and accurately, leading to rapid extraction of actionable intelligence crucial for decision-making and operational planning. This enables military commanders to anticipate and respond to emerging threats more effectively. Quantum computing and cryptology permit the securing of data, enhance resilience and security and empower military forces to harness the full potential of data to gain a competitive edge in future conflicts. The competition for Data superiority is termed an 'Algorithm War' and refers to the competition to develop and deploy advanced algorithms in military, economic and societal domains. It reflects the increasing importance of algorithms as a critical resource.

Transition from NCW to DCW

NCW is all about the interconnectivity of systems, real-time exchange of data, and developing robust communication architecture to enhance info availability for enhancing collaboration, joint operations and rapid response to changing situations. On the other hand, DCW emphasises the primacy of data as a strategic asset for effective decision-making. Thus, DCW architecture is required to be adopted to enhance operational effectiveness. The concept of NCW is based on 'Info Superiority' through rapid sharing and integration of information across military networks, whereas DCW relies on 'Decision Superiority', prioritising the effective analysis, interpretation and exploitation of data to enable informed decision-making. It allows military forces to anticipate threats, seize opportunities and maintain a competitive advantage on the modern battlefield. Therefore, one can conclude that while NCW will result in superiority in one Domain, DCW would facilitate superiority in a domain (System of systems)' through a 'Faster OODA loop'.

Taking the concept to its extreme, Data-Centric Warfare (DCW) could potentially lead to human beings being 'out of the loop' as autonomous systems, driven by advanced algorithms and AI, assume greater control over decision-making and operations.

Celerity Centric Warfare

This segment is being driven by advances in hypersonics, Stealth, lethal autonomous systems and long-range precision guidance. These technologies enable faster, more elusive and highly precise strikes across all domains, including underwater and space, thus reshaping the strategic landscape and influencing the future of military operations and deterrence strategies. The convergence of drones and loitering munitions (with smaller radar cross sections and moving slowly), cruise missiles, ballistic missiles, quasi-ballistic missiles, Fractional Orbit Bombardment Systems (FOBS) – hypersonic missiles, hypersonic glide vehicles (HGVs) are reshaping modern warfare. These systems offer rapid deployment, precise targeting and reduced response times, challenging traditional defence mechanisms and escalating the speed and lethality of conflicts. AD planning against saturation attacks by a combination of sub, super and hypersonic weapons will become increasingly challenging due to the proliferation of these advanced technologies among state and non-state actors. These new-age weapons may also make large platforms increasingly vulnerable to coordinated saturated attacks.

Counters to these systems should incorporate advanced sensors, rapid response capabilities and layered defences to detect, track and neutralise multiple threats simultaneously. Additionally, investments in counter-drone technologies, directed energy weapons and enhanced electronic warfare capabilities are essential to enhance the survivability of large platforms in modern conflict scenarios. A weapon system that is unaudible, untrackable and undetectable is going to be untargetable.

Info-Centric Warfare

Info-centric warfare is waged primarily in the cognitive domain, focusing on influencing perceptions, beliefs and behaviours through information and communication strategies. Also known as 'Influence Operations', it aims to shape the decision-making processes of adversaries, friendly nations and populations by leveraging various means such as propaganda, psychological operations and strategic communications, thereby shaping the outcomes of modern conflicts. Propaganda, misinformation, deceit and ruse have long been integral elements of warfare, dating back to ancient times. In the ancient Indian epic, the Mahabharata, 'Aswathama hatha iti Narova Kunjarova' was declared by none other than Yudhishtra to disarm Dronacharya. He was the most credible source of information. Similarly, Lord Krishna employed deception during the battle of Kurukshetra by orchestrating an illusory twilight, making Jayadratha believe that night had fallen.

With the proliferation of the internet, social media and digital communication platforms, Information is increasingly being weaponised as a tool to influence minds and shape opinions. Through the manipulation of narratives, dissemination of propaganda and spread of misinformation, actors with vested interests, social media platforms, online forums and news outlets are congregating to weaponise information to wage psychological warfare. Sentiment analysis, social influencers and fake news are rapidly emerging as critical tools in an evolving concept of information warfare. Meanwhile, fake news continues to spread misinformation and propaganda to sow confusion and undermine trust in traditional sources of information. Together, these elements form a potent arsenal in the battle for information dominance.

In contemporary warfare, matrices of victory (Perception of Victory) are not solely determined by battlefield outcomes but are equally influenced by perceptions in the cognitive domain. The human mind becomes the battleground where narratives, propaganda and psychological operations shape beliefs, attitudes and behaviours. Therefore, mastering the cognitive domain is essential for achieving strategic objectives.

War of Convergence

The increasing capabilities of Information and non-contact warfare are having a significant impact on how warfare is being viewed, taught and executed. To effectively encompass the complexities of these RMA in contemporary times, an attempt has been made to term the 3rd RMA as the 'Convergence Warfare' as it converges the following:

- 1st and 2nd RMA with the 3rd.
- Data Centric, Celerity Centric and Info-Centric Warfare.
- Kinetic with non-kinetic – including cognitive/critical thinking.
- Time and Space.
- Emerging and disruptive technologies like AI, ML, hypersonic, quantum, deep learning automotive platforms etc.
- Tactics with Operational Art and War Strategy.

Convergence will allow integration of all Elements of National Power including the Armed Forces with due alacrity in the continuum of a Crisis – Confrontation – Conflict and Combat. The defining features of the third RMA will be innovation, cognitive load-sharing between man and machine, machine-level decisions and actions and finally an enhancement of net-centricity (one may call it web or mesh centricity). In the future, nations and militaries are likely to work towards the achievement of better information, improved understanding and effective decision-making through faster assessment of outcomes. However, this intent will require not only technological absorption but also thought transformation and organisational reorientations.

Contemporary Application of the 3rd RMA

This technological convergence featuring emerging and disruptive technologies indicates a shift towards the third Revolution in Military Affairs (RMA). We are witnessing aspects of this in the ongoing Russia-Ukraine conflict. Innovation in the military domain, such as the use of the Saker Scout drone in autonomous mode by the Ukrainians, illustrates the convergence of Emerging & Disruptive Technologies (EDTs) with manoeuvre warfare. Additionally, companies like Palantir, Maxar and Clearview have respectively provided products like sensor and data fusion, satellite imagery and analysis and facial recognition technology to the Ukrainians. Drones and long-range missiles have been used in conjunction by the Russians to attack Ukrainian civilian and military infrastructure while unmanned surface vessels (USVs) have targeted the Russian fleet in the Black Sea. The effective use of USVs in a strategic maritime theatre exemplifies the crucial role of technology mastery over data, infrastructure, algorithms and talent in modern warfare.

Conclusion

As we look back, how technology has contributed to the evolution of warfare making it diverse, expansive, high–paced, lethal, precise, integrated and inter-connected, is evident. As we analyse the evolving spectrum of technology, it is possible to visualise the complexities of the manner, domains through which it will be conducted and the targets for future wars. While 'Multi-Domain Operations (MDO)' will become inevitable, flexible and sophisticated, the response through the Entire Continuum' of crisis-confrontation-conflict-combat will become a necessity. Additionally, 'Integrated Rapid Response' by utilising a mix of contact and non-contact along with kinetic and non-kinetic means will provide the desired results. 'Adaptive organisations' absorbing and leveraging EDTs will become a reality in future.

India is at the cusp of great change and correct actions at this stage are necessary to build the core of technological strength within the nation. We have laid down our path to become a 'Viksit and Shashakt Bharat'. A correct approach by the defence ecosystem during these times will ensure that we can transform our thoughts, skills and capabilities that are essential for building a 'Future Ready Armed Forces'.

Section C

REFORMS

9

Jointness and Integration 2.0

> *"Integration and jointness among the armed forces are vital to enhance their operational efficiency and prepare them for future challenges. We are committed to developing joint structures and operational strategies to create a more cohesive and effective defence force."*
>
> —RM Rajnath Singh

Introduction

The Cabinet note that approved the creation of the post of the Chief of Defence Staff (CDS) as well as the Department of Military Affairs (DMA) in the Ministry of Defence (MoD) states that one of the aims and objectives of reforms in the Higher Defence Management in India is 'to bring about jointness' between the armed forces. It also mentions that the mandate of DMA is to "promote jointness in procurement, training, staffing through Joint Planning and Integration of the requirements". Two distinct activities are being envisaged, one a tangible and physical activity of 'bringing jointness' and the other more abstract of 'promoting jointness'.

"Jointness" can be described as 'Cross Service Cooperation' in all stages of military processes from research through procurement to operations. We also find that the word 'Joint' is prefixed to several activities, products and processes like Joint Planning, Joint Capabilities, Joint Training, Joint Operations, Joint Doctrines, Joint Directives etc. I believe, all these 'Joint' activities are predicated on a mindset of jointness prevailing in the environment for that activity, process or product to achieve its desired aims and objectives. Jointness lies in a psychological or nonphysical domain, a bonding with something intangible and abstract.

Achieving and understanding Jointness was key and therefore it needed to be clearly articulated. Jointness was explained as being synonymous with an environment where trust prevails among members of the three services. The purpose of Jointness is to create a congenial working environment where we can discuss new ideas without fear or apprehension and propose novel approaches to bring efficiency without prejudice. Bonhomie, trust and openness are the basic building blocks for laying the foundation of 'Jointness'. Jointness can also be seen as the sine qua non for 'Integration' which had been described as a physical activity. Several verticals like operations, intelligence, planning, operational logistics, communications, training, inventory and supply chain management, administration, HR issues and legal matters have also been identified for integration. These two activities "Jointness and Integration" are important prerequisites for the creation of joint operational structures including Joint Theatre Commands.

History of Jointness

The need for Jointness among the three services was recognised by the political and military leadership of the newly independent India very early. A Joint Services Wing was created at Clement Town, Dehradun, a precursor to the National Defence Academy that came up at Khadakwasla, Pune. However, the divide between the services grew as officers of each service grew in a closed environment of their respective service, imbibing a culture of their own. This is a natural phenomenon and not unique to the Indian Armed Forces alone. After all, officers are motivated to join a particular service owing to several reasons such as distinct uniforms, organisational histories, battle accounts or the traditions and work environment that a particular service offers. As young officers grow, they are seeped into a particular culture and view all matters from the perspective of the Service they belong to. Their knowledge of other services and their utility is restricted due to inadequate interaction and exposure, reinforcing a prejudiced mindset. Officers progress in their careers constantly looking at all issues from a prism influenced by the colour of the uniform they don.

- There is hardly any institutionalised mechanism in the Indian Armed Forces to bridge this divide. The Defence Services Staff College (DSSC) was designated as a tri-services institution, but apart from being located together, no training for joint operations or efforts to develop a joint culture takes place. The three services trained separately under their respective Chief Instructors with few joint tutorials and some relevant joint content.
- The three War Colleges that groom the officers of the armed forces for undertaking higher responsibilities are located in different geographies of the Country. Their syllabus has evolved to take care of operations of their Service with little emphasis on joint operations. JOCAP does bring officers undergoing training at Service Specific War Colleges together for a capsule of five weeks but that is inadequate by any standards that evaluate the depth of integration required amongst the three Services. At best, it can provide a basic understanding of joint operations. It does not contribute to the development of a Joint Culture.

Differences between the services also got accentuated due to several other reasons, primarily due to competition over sharing of meagre defence allocation for building individual service capabilities. The Service Chiefs being responsible to the government for tackling any threat in their respective domains, meant that no service felt that it should be found wanting in times of crisis. Differences at the apex level gradually permeated to the rank and file of each service. Unfortunately, this was encouraged so that the three services do not present a united front.

The unbridgeable nature of differences between the three services was witnessed during the peacekeeping operations in Sri Lanka in 'Op Pawan' and the Kargil War in 'Op Vijay'. Future challenges to the Armed Forces may not be limited to sub-conventional domains or limited conflict. The Armed Forces must prepare themselves from a 'maximalist threat perspective'. The future, it is well known, beckons a net-centric integrated response in a multi-domain environment.

Jointness 2.0: The Concept

Jointness is essentially a mindset. Being in the psychological or nonphysical domain, it is difficult to measure the levels of its effectiveness. Jointness has gained quite a lot of traction and has been received very well amongst service members wearing the three uniforms. There is also a growing sense of self-realisation that it is an idea that we should have implemented some time ago. No major differences among the Services have surfaced in 2023 encouraging the services to move towards the next level of Jointness – Jointness 2.0.

Jointness 2.0 is about developing a 'Joint Culture' in our armed forces. There are three Service Specific Cultures in our Armed Forces. Even in Joint Service Organisations, officers come with the baggage of their services. There is a need, therefore, to create a fourth culture in the armed forces, a "Joint Culture". This is essential as we move towards creating Joint Operational Structures. The joint organisations including Joint/ Theatre Commands, will succeed only once they unleash their capabilities 'Jointly'.

Joint Culture: A Framework

Culture is a way of life for a group of people. It is the total of their beliefs and values and manifests in a particular pattern of behaviour. Developing a culture takes time and it must be passed down to successive generations for it to survive and grow.

In the Air Force, there is a culture of professionalism among fighter pilots since they are training for combat every day. This is an excellent virtue. However, skill in flying is considered so important that sometimes professional growth on larger aspects of national security or military application gets neglected. The officers of the Indian Navy have a strategic perspective because of the nature of their job. A Navy man feels that he is a 'sailor diplomat' because the nature of the Navy's employment has diplomacy embedded into it. The Army feels that metrics of victory will always be measured by the number of boots on the ground. The large monolithic organisation is so steeped in customs and traditions that it takes time for information to percolate down through multiple filters, both organisational and cultural.

The Joint Culture, though different from a Service Specific Culture, needs to respect the uniqueness of each service. We must be able to distill the best of each service and incorporate the Highest Common Factor, rather than settling for the Least Common Denominator. The Joint Culture must promote originality in thought – the thinking process. Certain ingredients of 'Joint Culture' have been identified as enunciated in the succeeding paragraphs.

Ingredients of a Joint Culture

Joint Culture though different from Service Specific Culture, needs to respect the uniqueness of each service. Certain ingredients of 'Joint Culture' have been identified as enunciated in the succeeding paragraphs.

- ***Original Thinking.*** The creation of the fourth culture in the Services – 'the Joint Culture' needs to be evolved based on new concepts, doctrines and tactics. Original thinking is essential to create an enabling framework that will distil the best of each service, and incorporate the Highest Common Factor, rather than settle for the Least Common Denominator.
- ***Sharing of Knowledge.*** Power comes not from hoarding information but from sharing it. Seamless sharing of knowledge and ideas both vertically and horizontally must be a signpost of Joint Culture. The tendency of protecting the 'knowledge turf' as this may lead to loss of perceived power and credit must be discouraged. Instead, a culture of openness must not only be encouraged but also incentivised.
- ***Innovative, Inventive, Imaginative and Indigenous (4Is).*** Our mythologies propound a concept of 'Creative Destruction' – to create something new, we need to discard the old. This concept is aptly suited for infusing the Joint Culture. There is a requirement to shed what may not be relevant and seek a new approach and direction to evolve. Adoption of the 4Is approach:

Innovative, Inventive, Imaginative and Indigenous is considered essential in this endeavour.

- ***Receptivity to Ideas.*** As is often said 'Communication is a two-way process', wherein, receptivity to other's opinions and ideas plays a very important part. We have all been groomed within service-specific norms, inspired by its unique traditions and values. Hence, it is very difficult to view constructive criticism with an impartial lens. 'Joint Culture' must aim to encourage 'receptivity to divergent viewpoints' and encourage professional debates. 'Joint Culture' should promote the ideology of "What is being said is important, rather than who has said it".
- ***Non-Hierarchal Staff Work.*** Our services have a defined hierarchical structure for seeking approvals on proposals. Whilst, there are advantages of the existing system in terms of 'checks and balances', it does suffer from the drawback of a finite amount of delays. The issue gets further aggravated, when the same cycle, post-Service HQ approval, has to be repeated within the HQ IDS. Therefore, the need of the hour is to establish horizontal structures that cut down this inordinate delay. A non-hierarchical structure for staff work is, therefore, being evolved for the promotion of Joint Culture.

Joint Culture: Symbology and Rituals

Symbology is a powerful tool to foster a sense of belonging among the members of an organisation, it gives them something tangible to identify with and rally behind – flags, badges, bespoke martial music, commemorative days and events are a few such symbolic aspects that can help to promote a joint culture. Rituals are traditions of a community that are carried out in a prescribed manner during formal events. Along with symbology, rituals help bind a community/group. To introduce and speed up the imbibing of a Joint Culture, there is a need to take the aid of symbology and rituals based on events, products and processes. Some of the ideas that could be taken forward are as follows:

- ***Annual Joint Conferences.*** These will be akin to Conferences of C-in-Cs held regularly and may be a precursor to possible conferences of Theatre Commanders. The heads of all Inter-Service Organisations, Joint Service Training Institutions and Commands (Andaman & Nicobar and SFC) must participate in these conferences.
- ***Conference of Joint Committees.*** A bi-annual conference of various Joint Sub-Committees of COSC must be held to lay down targets for Jointness & Integration and to review the progress.
- ***Showcasing Integration.*** A day would be earmarked as 'Integration Day' to celebrate the unity of effort achieved by Tri-Service cooperation and cohesion, which will also be represented through a tableau for the Republic Day Parade 2025. DSSC will take out a magazine on 'Jointness and Integration', which could also be the theme of professional journals of not only tri-service training institutes but also those of Service/Arm specific journals.
- ***Joint Training.*** Training at DSSC must include a separate group that undergoes Joint Training for the complete year. The feedback from such an experiment could be taken forward for larger implementation.

The foot soldiers for creating the Joint Culture are the officers posted to the Tri-Service Institutions and HQ. They are the starting points for developing trust, camaraderie, bonhomie and understanding – foundations for 'Jointness' and will pave the way for a 'future war ready' Indian Armed Forces.

Integration

The conjoining or bringing together of two diverse entities or organisations is called integration. It is a physical activity which is apparent, visible and objectively measured. The integration combines the unique capabilities of each service through a process of creation of a structure to increase the warfighting capability and efficiency of the system. The integration will lead to the optimisation of the resources concerning manpower, infrastructure and time through reengineering of processes and reorganising. It must be understood that optimisation is not the aim behind Integration but a result of a process of introducing efficiency. Integration is a prerequisite to the creation of Theatre Commands and lies between the amorphous state of Jointness and the end state of a functional Theatre Command.

The verticals, in the order of priority, considered essential for integration before the establishment of Theatre Commands are communications, operations, intelligence, training, operational logistics, HR, legal, administration and maintenance & services.

Integration 2.0

In 2023, a large number of activities, events, exercises and initiatives were attempted to bring about greater integration among the three services. Exercise Vayu Shakti saw the participation of the Indian Army and Indian Air Force aviation platforms. Exercise Bharat Shakti demonstrated the tri-service application of indigenous platforms in an integrated/networked environment. Several exercises were planned at the level of Command HQ and below. Cross-postings of several officers took place. While all these activities exemplified a good beginning and made a positive impact, the endurance of the effect of such stand-alone events was felt to be short-lived. All efforts for integration must flow from a policy or directive. The effort must be encapsulated in a formal instruction or order to make it visible. Integration 2.0 envisages the issue of several Joint Instructions, Joint Orders and Joint Policies/Directives. These will be arrived at through a consultative process for implementation.

- ***Joint Instructions.*** These issues have financial and legal implications like Conditions of Service (Joint Staff), Pay and Allowances, Scaling of Equipment, Financial Powers and Procedures etc.
- ***Joint Orders.*** To be issued post approval of Secretary DMA, they have legal implications. These orders will be applicable for all Joint Service Organisations and three Services. Joint Orders, if

issued under the aegis of HQ IDS, would be applicable for Tri-Service Organisations/Establishments only.

- ***Joint Policy Directives.*** These do not have the authority of an order but need to be implemented by the Section/Branch/HQ. These may be issued at the level of DMA or HQ IDS, as applicable.

Conclusion

Jointness and Integration are important in case we have to establish Joint Theatre Commands and graduate our capabilities for multi-domain operations in a net-centric environment. We have lost time but need to realise that not only are these an essential element of reforms but also required for speeding up the process. 'There is no defined End State' to Jointness and Integration. It is a continuous process and will continue even after the establishment of Joint/Theatre Commands.

10

HDO: Past, Present and Future

> *"The higher defence organization in India has been evolving continuously to meet emerging challenges. We are committed to integrating our defence strategies with modern technologies and strengthening our operational capabilities to ensure national security and strategic autonomy."*
>
> —RM Rajnath Singh

Introduction

The need for a robust Higher Defence Organisation (HDO) for India arises from the nature of threats and challenges it faces in the maritime and aerospace domains and disputed land borders in the form of the Line of Control (LC) and the Line of Actual Control (LAC). One of the most important functions of HDO is to ensure military preparedness of the highest order and provide clear directions to the armed forces in times of crisis. Equally important is a distinct vision for the development of long-term capabilities based on a realistic assessment of the emerging regional and global security environment. India aspires to be a developed nation by 2047. It is also on the path to becoming the third-largest economy by 2030. Keeping in step with its rising economic profile, there is a need to create a robust yet flexible defence architecture with commensurate military capabilities and a system to provide overarching strategic guidance.

The creation of the post of the Chief of Defence Staff (CDS) and the Department of Military Affairs (DMA) in 2020 is the first set of reforms initiated in recent times by the government to streamline the HDO in India. This initiative intends to provide the necessary impetus to promote jointness amongst the three services, and integrate their existing operations, logistics and human resource (HR) structures, besides creating the desired momentum for the inception of Joint/Integrated Theatre Commands. It is just the beginning and can be seen as a stepping-stone to usher in the next generation of reforms in the armed forces and their governing structures. To crystal gaze into the future, it is essential to look at the past to understand the origins of HDO in India and its evolution to the present.

Evolution of HDO: The Past

Post-independence, the basic structures adopted for forming HDO for India were based on the recommendations of Lord Lionel Ismay, the Chief of Staff of Lord Louis Mountbatten, the first Governor General of independent India. Lord Ismay recommended a three-tiered HDO, approved by the Cabinet in Oct 1947. It comprised of the following:

- A Defence Committee of the Cabinet (DCC) to be chaired by the Prime Minister (PM). The DCC was originally assigned to have the Defence Minister, Commanders-in-Chief (Cs-in-C) and the Defence Secretary as its members. However, direct access of the Cs-in-C to the Government was ruled out because the initial few Cs-in-C were British officers. The custom continued even when Cs-in-C/Chief of Staff appointments were held by Indian officers.
- The Defence Minister Committee (DMC) chaired by the Defence Minister.
- A Chiefs of Staff Committee (COSC) under the chairmanship of Field Marshal KM Cariappa, the then C-in-C. This was formed to provide advice on service matters to the Defence Minister and through him to the DCC. Later the chairmanship of COSC was made rotational with the longest-serving Chief of the committee becoming its Chairman.

Lord Ismay, while recommending this organisational structure, also suggested several sub-committees functioning under the COSC to bring jointness in training, intelligence, logistics administration etc. This led to the creation of the Military Wing under the already existing Deputy Secretary (Military) in the Cabinet Secretariat for secretarial support to the COSC and its sub-committees. The Deputy Secretary (Military) had a distinct task of advising the Cabinet Secretary in matters dealing with inter-ministerial matters such as defence. For example, one of the major tasks was the handling and regular updation of the Union War Book and through it, the preparation and necessary coordination for the execution of war. The Military Wing was given the additional task of providing the secretariat to the DCC, DMC and the COSC and their various sub-committees. This organisational arrangement enabled the Military Wing to keep the Cabinet Secretary updated regarding important defence developments. The Military Wing, therefore, functioned as a bridge between the Cabinet Secretary and through him the Cabinet on one side, and the Defence Ministry and Chiefs of Staff on the other about higher defence issues.

India became a Republic on 26 Jan 1950 and the mantle of the supreme commander-in-chief of the nation's armed forces was now vested in the President of India. The nomenclature of service chiefs was changed from Cs-in-C to Chiefs of Staff, though they retained their operational role and responsibilities. In July 1952, when the Allocation of Business (AoB) and Transaction of Business (ToB) rules were promulgated, the three service HQs became "attached offices" of the Ministry of Defence (MoD) rather than being part of it. Their responsibilities were restricted to executing and overseeing the implementation of policies laid down by the government and advising the government on technical aspects.

The next major transformation happened in 1961 through an amendment to the ToB rules when the responsibility of the country's defence was placed on the shoulders of the defence secretary. The service chiefs could now access DMC/Raksha Mantri (RM) only in an advisory capacity. Politico-military linkages were further narrowed down. The

Military Wing could now access the political leadership/CCPA only through the Cabinet Secretariat. Under this arrangement, there remained a possibility, even if theoretical, to take up a matter with the Cabinet Committee on Political Affairs (CCPA)/Cabinet, even if it was negated by the Ministry of Defence (MoD). However, even this possibility was foreclosed. The last delinking, which closed the window completely, was the transfer of the Military Wing of the Cabinet Secretariat to the MoD. This shift also led to some COSC committees becoming dormant and certain organisations like the Defence Research and Development Organisation (DRDO), Director General of Quality Assurance (DGQA) and Directorate of Standardisation being disconnected from the users i.e. the Service HQ.

The evolution of COSC as the highest decision-making body dates back to 1947. Its main function was to advise the Defence Minister and, through him, the DCC on all matters meriting ministerial consideration. It has a well-defined role, both in peace and war. During war, it advises the government on issues like mobilisation, the role of reservists and the declaration of emergency whereas during peace, it advises on defence policies/strategy, force structuring and threat assessment. The COSC had some inherent drawbacks like disproportionate tenures of the Chairman and challenges in arriving at impartial decisions by the Chairman COSC because of the dichotomy between his role as the head of a service and thus being responsible for any challenges to national security emerging in that domain (land, sea or air) and that of discharging his responsibility for the overall capability development of the armed forces. There was always a push-pull dynamic in the workings of the COSC.

The Kargil War brought to the fore shortcomings in the HDO. Post the Kargil Committee Report, the Group of Ministers (GoM) headed by Arun Singh, constituted to bring in reforms in HDO, recommended the creation of the post of CDS and Vice Chief of Defence Staff (VCDS), besides creating an Integrated Defence Staff HQ (IDS). However, what emerged was the HQ of IDS and the post of Chief of IDS to Chairman COSC (CISC), generally regarded as a suboptimal measure. The creation of the new structure under CISC was aimed at strengthening jointness and building synergy amongst the armed forces. However, the reforms neither enhanced the role of the COSC nor gave requisite powers to HQ IDS to carry out its mandated functions. The Defence Planning Staff (DPS), which was supposedly the bridge between COSC and MoD was also subsumed under HQ IDS, eliminating the last link between the MoD and COSC.

The Present HDO

There were a lot of debates and deliberations on reforms in HDO, especially concerning the appointment of the CDS. It was only after 18 years of establishment of HQ IDS that the government finally took the plunge in August 2019, when the PM announced the creation of the post of CDS from the ramparts of Red Fort on Independence Day. He said,

> "Our country has been debating for a long about reforms in Armed Forces and many commissions and their reports underline the same. To further sharpen coordination between the forces, India will have a Chief of Defence Staff, CDS which will make the forces even more effective".

The creation of the post of CDS was aimed to organically fit into the higher defence management of the country. This was followed by a commensurate accretion in the responsibilities and powers for enabling the CDS to effectively and objectively fulfil his role and responsibilities. To accomplish this, the government also created the Department of Military Affairs (DMA) within the MoD with specific roles and responsibilities. AoB and ToB Rules were amended to split the responsibility between the Department of Defence (DoD) and DMA. The basic principle of division of responsibilities between the DoD and DMA lies in segregating the larger defence overview (still with DoD) from purely military matters (now under DMA).

The creation of DMA in the MoD was a step which fused the civil and military structures, providing unity in thought and action on defence-related matters at ministerial levels. Never before were military officers given secretarial powers. With the creation of DMA, the military has once again got a formal representation within the MoD with sufficient discretionary powers. The creation of the CDS and the DMA has been a transformative change with the CDS now wearing three hats – that of the CDS, Secretary DMA and Permanent Chairman of COSC. The creation of such a post also removed the drawbacks of the existing system. The rotational nature of the appointment of Chairman COSC resulted in disproportionate tenures and interest in joint operations being overshadowed by service-specific requirements. A Permanent Chairman of COSC now provides continuity and an unbiased approach towards tri-services matters. The CDS provides a single point of advice to the government as the principal military advisor and as head of tri-services organisations, ensuring effective control over integrated functions. The CDS's parallel appointment as Secretary DMA ensures that the military is now part of governmental decision-making at the apex level.

The Future HDO for India

The CCS note that approved the creation of the post of CDS and DMA, laid down specific deliverables related to enhancing jointness and integration within the Indian armed forces, leading to the establishment of Joint theatre commands. This transformational path requires the Indian armed forces to undertake reforms in organisation, structures, concepts/ doctrines and culture. It would result in a major reorientation of existing processes and the creation of new joint structures. These would be revolutionary and transformative attempts with far-reaching implications. It would not only result in revised command and control arrangements with lower formation functions but also transform the decision-making within the overall HDO hierarchy.

The present transformation is being attempted through a three-stage process of jointness, integration and theaterisation. These three issues are closely linked with each other but when viewed individually, have a different meaning. Theaterisation can only happen when there is a sufficient amount of integration amongst the three services, while integration can only happen when there is jointness-based bonding between them. With theaterisation as a goal for the end state, it has to be seen as an evolved form of integration from an operational perspective involving the creation of joint tri-service theatre-specific structures for effective response along the entire spectrum of conflict. These theatre-specific structures would be responsible for the planning, coordination and conduct of military operations in their area of responsibility. It is an attempt to replace the existing structure for the management of operations with a more efficient one. The transformational change will take time for establishment and stabilisation and hence will be difficult to fathom in its entirety but will impact most of the peace and war time functions of the armed forces including HDO and the decision-making process.

In the domain of HDO, the process of planning, preparation and conducting of war consists of multiple deliberations at various levels of decision-making. These are borne out of consultative processes both within the military and between the civilian and military leadership. Further, several additional and important activities will have linkages between the military, other ministries and the gamut of civilian agencies responsible for various aspects of national security. These activities will be required to be undertaken to brief the CCS and seek strategic direction to evolve strategic plans. Some of the changes that may occur in the HDO structure to support the concept of Joint Theatre Commands are as follows:

- Separation of responsibility for 'force employment' from 'force generation'. The former will rest with theatre commanders and the latter with Service chiefs. This inter alia measure also means that Service chiefs will have to shed their operational roles and responsibilities.
- Creation of Joint Structures for operations, intelligence and operational logistics functions by amalgamating the establishments currently responsible in Service HQ for the same.
- Service HQ would undergo massive organisational changes to realise the true integration at the levels of Joint HQ and Theatre

Commands. There would be a need to establish clear-cut linkages between SHQs and HDO on one hand and to theatre commands on the other.

- A relook at the composition and role of COSC and various sub-committees under it will be required. Some of the sub-committees like JOCOM etc will no longer be required.
- Integrating the new domains of warfare like cyber and space into the existing domains and finalising the requisite operational and functional linkages between them.

In the revised organisational structure, it is envisaged that the service chiefs would continue to be advisors to the Government on service-specific matters, while operational matters will be in the domain of Theatre Commanders. The CDS will continue to be the single-point military advisor to the RM/government. There will be other challenges in HDO reforms. At the apex level, these reforms will be broad-based, however, on the ground, there are hierarchal challenges and HR-related issues which are complex and will need to be addressed. Similarly, the principle of chain of command and operational decision matrix will also need to be redefined. Finally, the necessity of all organs of defence machinery like DMA, DoD, Service HQ and Theatre Commands functioning in perfect harmony is sine qua non to achieve higher HDO goals.

Conclusion

It is a difficult task to run large organisations like the Armed Forces. Even routine matters are complex and time-consuming since the stakes are always high. There is no room for error. To train, motivate and keep an army of 12 lakhs operationally ready is not an easy task. Similarly, exploiting technologically intensive platforms and maintaining them is a major challenge for the IAF and Indian Navy. After 75 years of independence, national security, defence and military reforms in the cognitive domain/mind space seem to be ready, more than ever before, for some decisive forward movement. During these times, the Indian Armed Forces must adopt a progressive approach towards military transformation as a means to achieve the end of building a future-ready Indian armed forces.

11

Atmanirbharta in Defence

> *"Our resolution for a self-reliant India is not inward looking. The idea behind making a strong India is to make the global economy more resilient and stable, and for the global peace."*
>
> —PM Narendra Modi

Introduction

The Indian Armed Forces, the second largest in the world, has long been a leading importer of military equipment. Recent wars, conflicts and black swan events have shown, that over-dependence on foreign suppliers for military platforms, support systems and technology can critically affect India's operational preparedness and war-waging potential due to uncertain supply chains and indeterminate motives of private and state actors. The only solution is 'Self-reliance' in defence production and innovation.

In the year 2020, the Hon'ble PM raised a clarion call to the nation through an 'Atmanirbhar Bharat Abhiyan', a Self-reliant India Campaign. It was an ambitious vision which succeeded the 'Make in India Initiative'. The latter was meant to propel the economic growth of the nation by making the country self-reliant in manufacturing, e-commerce and IT services. The Atmanirbhar initiative now aims to propel India towards achieving strategic autonomy through economic self-reliance and technological innovation. One needs to emphasise here that self-reliance or Atmanirbharta is not a vision of autarky as some fear. The vision of self-reliance is that of a strong and prosperous India which acts as a friend to the world community at large (Vishvamitra). It is the blueprint for the Viksit Bharat of 2047.

Atmanirbharta: Concept and Inspirations

The roots of Atmanirbharta run deep in the fabric of India's ancient culture. India has long been a reservoir of original thoughts, knowledge, wisdom and innovation spread across multiple domains and disciplines. India introduced zero and the decimal system to the world and encouraged the development of new ideas and thoughts in the fields of knowledge, strategic thinking, astrology, astronomy, mathematics, medicine and surgery, among others, that later became the base for new inventions and innovations across the globe. Ancient India had a rich heritage, abundant wealth, intellectual heft, an all-embracing confluence of religions, traditions & customs and most importantly, a spirit of self-reliance.

The words 'Atman' in Atmanirbharta and 'Self' in Self-Reliance point towards an understanding of the self. It underscores the idea of self-realisation that will then lead to self-confidence and self-actualisation. Atmanirbharta aims to instil pride amongst Indian citizens in the country's culture, traditional thoughts, and ideas and infuse a sense of confidence in the nation's capabilities. The Vishwa Guru of yesteryears should look within for inspirational sources. Atmanirbharta is a philosophy that encourages confidence in own abilities.

As a philosophy, Atmanirbharta is much more than industrial manufacturing. It is a vision of understanding India's present to create a new culture of self-confidence, based on inspiration from the past. Atmanirbharta has special relevance for the Armed Forces since it will impact not only own weapons and equipment but also new concepts of warfighting. Its mandate and scope are much larger and have to be viewed in a larger context beyond the narrow confines of defence manufacturing.

In the field of defence manufacturing, Atmanirbharta can be considered as the next iteration of 'Make in India'. While 'Make in India' is a technology and country agnostic (the intention is to project the country as the world's factory as well as encourage innovation and technology absorption through the transfer of technology and incentivising foreign manufacturers to set shop here), Atmanirbharta focuses on owning the entire inception-conception-validation-scaling-action (ICVSA) cycle i.e. achieving sovereignty over the development life of a product from conceptualisation to development, it's marketing, its exploitation, upgrade and eventual replacement with yet another technologically superior product. In short, it calls for a revamp of the overall system to enhance Indian capacity and capabilities.

Atmanirbharta has sometimes been interpreted as an isolationist mindset, where India seeks to shield itself from external influences. However, 'Atmanirbharta' aims to attain self-sustainability and share Indian skills, services and products for the betterment and development of the world at large to make a greater contribution globally. In its overall efforts for global betterment, India seeks global partnerships as well. Even the 'Make in India' initiatives encourage foreign participation and collaborative effort by the establishment of Joint Ventures (JVs). Atmanirbharata would look at co-development and co-production.

Atmanirbharta and the Indian Military

The fighting prowess of Armed Forces comprises three main attributes i.e., conceptual, physical and moral. Conceptual prudence is a major factor which plays an important role in bringing clarity and thoughts through the development of strategies, doctrines and military tactics. Physical assets are instruments of warfighting including weapons, equipment, infrastructure and systems. The morale of the Armed Forces emanates from their fighting spirit which is a product of the high standards of training, discipline, confidence and self-belief. Historical evidence indicates that Armed forces led with conceptual clarity, superior physical assets and high morale have won engagements with their adversaries. One believes that conceptual clarity contributes more towards winning. This aspect of Atmanirbharta in the development of conceptual constructs assumes greater importance in an environment of global change and transformation.

Currently, the Indian military is heavily reliant on foreign equipment and technology. A corollary to this is that Indian tactics is heavily drawn from Western ideas and bound with the limitations of their weapons systems which may or may not be optimised for Indian warfighting conditions or war aims. Therefore, Atmanirbharta has a very special meaning and relevance for the Armed Forces. Dependence on foreign products, platforms, systems and borrowed war-fighting concepts cannot be the foundation for a militarily strong India. Imported weapon systems and war-fighting concepts in times of crisis may not work optimally and also may deny us and deprive us of the very element of surprise. Accordingly, there is no alternative but to evolve and develop confidence in our abilities and develop requisite capabilities. It is more of a 'battle of minds' and 'mindset' change than physical capabilities. The conceptual mindscape change will shape the manufacturing landscape. It will be a slow process once the need has been established.

The foremost need for the armed forces is to accept that they can fight with indigenous weapons and systems. The Armed Forces need to promote Indian weapons and platforms and unless they are convinced of the changes, this initiative of Atmanirbharta will not succeed. To maintain their operational preparedness, armed forces need to be innovative and create alternate methods to reduce foreign dependency. They need to evolve new tactics to optimise the effectiveness of indigenous weapon systems.

Atmanirbharta in Defence Manufacturing

Military technology by nature is a complex field with a huge gestation period for its development. With the influx of disruptive niche technologies, the technology landscape has become even more complex. Today, the rate of obsolescence of technological products has become faster due to multiple innovations in the fields of digitisation, data analysis, miniaturisation and computation. In case, nations and organisations are not able to anticipate these changes and there is a lack of alternate technologies or platforms, it would be difficult for most of the nations to play the catch-up game, resulting in continued reliance on imports. Therefore, for India to become truly self-reliant in the defence sector, it would require a whole of the nation approach with every entity contributing towards creating an enabling environment to encourage active participation by both the public and private sector enterprises. The primacy has to be given to critical areas like aero engines, advance materials and manufacturing these and many more.

Defence manufacturing involves three stages i.e. Research & Development (R&D), Trial and Testing followed by serial production. Exploitation of the equipment, modifications and improvement follow. All three stages need to be reformed for a progressive approach towards indigenisation and innovation.

The defence R&D ecosystem, especially the DRDO needs a refocus and reorientation towards niche technologies. The large Science and Technology (S&T) talent pool of the country which includes the academia, the IITs and other S&T organisations along with their technology incubators and finally R&D by the private sector and DPSUs, needs to be brought in sync with the needs and requirements of the armed forces. The capability and capacity creation for R&D in cutting-edge niche technologies need no elaboration. We, as a nation, are blessed to have a young demographic profile with an adequate penchant for technical know-how. We can boast of reputed academic institutions like the IITs, IIITs, IIMs, etc. which have nurtured and provided world leaders in the field of technology and innovation. We must look at maximising their involvement in R&D through their active participation in select futuristic and niche capabilities to achieve and retain an edge over our adversaries.

One of the significant challenges faced by the Indian defence industry is the lack of a robust ecosystem and requisite trial and testing infrastructure. Atmanirbharta or self-reliance in the defence sector will essentially mean having sovereignty over defence products from R&D to serial production. Our defence industrial ecosystem needs to graduate to a level where Indian products become the most competitive and the preferred option for acquisition by foreign nations. Moreover, the mere size of our Armed Forces makes economic sense to produce defence equipment within the nation. The defence manufacturing ecosystem needs to transform from 'World Dependent' to 'Self Dependent', particularly in the areas of mass manufacturing with some capability to develop and manufacture advanced weapon platforms and systems in the initial stages.

Given the sheer size of our Armed Forces and the diverse range of capabilities we need to develop, there is a need to enhance the capacities of our manufacturing ecosystem. The involvement of the private sector augurs well for our capacity creation. I am sanguine that the emergence of the private sector in the design, development and manufacture of defence equipment would usher in healthy competition, joint ventures and Public-Private Partnership (PPP). In the domain of defence manufacturing, there is a need for a broader synergistic application between Tier II and Tier III MSMEs, DPSUs, the private sector, startups and even individual entrepreneurs and innovators. Here handholding and funding to bring an idea or concept up to the prototype level and steering it to the acquisition process has to be done proactively through schemes like iDEX, iDEX PRIME, ADITI and TDF.

Defence Manufacturing Initiatives and Impact

The policy announcement towards achieving 'Atmanirbharta in Defence' has been a big step towards self-reliance in the defence sector. It also offers a great opportunity for the Indian defence industry to use the occasion to manufacture items from the 'Positive Indigenisation List' by using their design & development or adopting technologies designed and developed by DRDO to meet the requirements of the Armed Forces. Today, the government is according to priority for the procurement of capital items from domestic sources under the Defence Acquisition Procedure (DAP-2020). Some of the initiatives are; the announcement of procurement of major defence platforms for the industry-led design and development, notification of Positive Indigenisation List (PIL), simplification of industrial licensing procedures with a longer validity period, liberalisation of FDI policies in defence, simplification of Make Procedure, corporatisation of OFBs, the launch of iDEX, TDF and ADITI schemes to spur innovations, reforms in offset policy, the launch of Srijan portal for import substitution and the establishment of Defence Industrial Corridor (DIC).

The primary aim of the policy reforms in the field of defence manufacturing is to unleash the entrepreneurial skills of Indians by broad-basing the innovation and indigenisation landscape. The green shoots of change are already visible with several Start-ups mushrooming and some graduating to become Unicorns. A ten-fold increase in defence exports is another indication of change.

Way Ahead

By adopting a multifaceted approach that combines technological innovations, collaborative frameworks and institutional reforms, India can pave the way for a more integrated and effective military, thereby ensuring the Nation's security in this increasingly complex geo-political landscape. Some of the concerns and ways ahead are mentioned in succeeding paragraphs.

- ***Family of Platforms.*** Our acquisition of weapon platforms/ equipment has been undertaken primarily to meet critical deficiencies and fill critical voids. Future acquisitions need to be aligned with our war-fighting concepts in consonance with futuristic battlefield requirements. There is also a case to compress our inventories by developing state-of-the-art weapon systems and 'Single Systems for Multiple Utility'. Inventory compression by inducting multi-utility weapon platforms has distinct advantages of interoperability, training, identification of friend and foe (IFF), and maintainability, besides conferring economic advantages.
- ***System Modularity.*** The concept of system modularity can provide flexibility not only in development and manufacturing but also in cutting down time and costs. To remain globally competitive, indigenous platform development needs to adopt system modularity as a concept. It breaks down complex systems and platforms into smaller sub-systems for design and development which can be used in larger platforms or even in a similar family of platforms.

- ***Import Substitution.*** Various initiatives are underway to indigenise the family of platforms required by the three services. Similar efforts are also being undertaken to indigenise assemblies/ sub-assemblies and spares of legacy platforms. A roadmap for Indigenisation with timelines has already been evolved for tanks, ammunition and Radar systems. A new chapter on Promoting Self-reliance through Indigenisation and Innovation has been included in the new Draft DPM-24, which is likely to be issued soon. Also, sustainment-related challenges are going to be taken up through the iDEX route.
- ***Tier II & III Suppliers.*** It is often argued that nations with a robust defence manufacturing ecosystem are dependent on several Tier II and Tier III suppliers located across the globe. Developed nations outsource defence manufacturing to other nations out of choice to cut down costs. For developing countries like India, going to foreign OEM is a compulsion and any compulsion is not a profitable venture. The shift from compulsion to choice is what India needs to aim for in the long run. This can only come about when we focus on the bottom of the Pyramid.
- ***Ammunition and Spares.*** There is a need to enhance capacities in the manufacturing of ammunition and spares for existing platforms. Currently, there is a huge shortage in the global availability of artillery ammunition, including rockets. This must be seen as an opportunity.
- ***Maintenance, Repair, and Overhaul (MRO) Hub for Foreign Platforms.*** As per global standards, the average life cycle cost of any military equipment is estimated to be three to four times the cost of its acquisition. There will be substantial revenue available to the Indian Defence Industry if MRO work is performed within the country. State-owned entities like Hindustan Aeronautics Limited (HAL), BEML and numerous shipyards, amongst other entities, have garnered substantial experience in implementing mid-life upgrades (MLUs) like transport aircraft, submarines,

helicopters, field guns and related ordnance. Thus, such an end-to-end sustainment ecosystem not only has the potential to make India an 'MRO Hub for the World', but also an export economy. India can provide substantial advancements by developing a sustainable end-to-end ecosystem for commercial, general and military MRO activities. With appropriate incentives, the private industry can play a crucial role in setup such facilities in Defence Industry Corridors through JVs/ToT with DPSUs/foreign OEMs. This would not only enable MRO of defence equipment of our Armed Forces but also facilitate India in becoming an 'MRO Hub for the world' in the long run.

Conclusion

The Indian PM's call for 'Atmanirbharta', amidst a global crisis of unprecedented scale and nature, has been one bold and astute. The demand for making India not just a large-scale market for the world but also a country that produces for the global market has been under discussion for the last many decades. This clarion call has the potential to turn the discussion into reality. GoI initiatives in the defence sector have shown commitment in terms of investment, policy and perseverance to undertake what it needs to make India an 'Atmanirbhar Bharat'. The journey, however, has just begun and is going to be long and arduous. The relevance of the 'Atmanirbharta in Defence' sector is the need of the future. It is up to us, the Armed Forces along with other GoI organisations and the Private Sector to chart an indigenous path towards 'Atmanirbharta' and self-reliance in defence.

12

Indigenisation and Innovation: The Road Ahead

"Innovation and indigenisation are important components, which are central to a strong and long-standing cooperation among the Armed Forces, Industry, R&D establishments, and academia. This collaboration is needed to achieve 'Aatmanirbharta' in defence and the overall goal of safety, security, and holistic development of the Nation."

—RM Rajnath Singh

Introduction

One of the major lessons of the Russia-Ukraine conflict and the Israel-Hamas war for India has been the need for diversification of its arms import base and the importance of self-reliance. Fortunately, the clarion call for Atmanirbharta by the Hon'ble PM was given much before the commencement of these conflicts and hence there prevailed a degree of awareness and acceptance of this concept. The two wars reinforced the idea of Atmanirbharta (or self-reliance) in a big way. Its importance for the nation's military preparedness as well as its virtue in maintaining strategic autonomy was now evident to most.

In the past, on occasions, India has experienced issues like human rights and other non-security related matters while attempting the import defence equipment. India's military preparedness cannot be held hostage to international power politics and pressures. Ideally, India should exercise sovereignty over the complete development cycle of weapon systems that it fields for its national security.

It is often said that in every disruption, there lies an opportunity. India since long been a major importer of arms and ammunition. The current flux in the global geo-political environment has forced most nations to review their national security strategies. A larger fiscal allocation for defence needs by most nations has led to a surge in demand for weapons and equipment that range from sophisticated air defence (AD) systems and missiles to relatively simpler 155mm artillery ammunition. India cannot be seen to be supporting any of the belligerents in the present conflicts or contributing directly to violence, destruction or loss of human life, but it can satisfy the needs of other nations which, like India, have been affected by disruption in the global supply chain of spares, arms, ammunition and attendant issues like maintenance, repair and overhaul (MRO) of equipment. It would help India to balance out its burgeoning import of defence equipment to some extent.

The road to strategic autonomy lies in self-reliance. However, no individual nation can ensure 100 per cent indigenous development of complex weapons platforms. Most nations follow a collaborative approach like in the case of sixth-generation fighter aircraft, the UK, Italy and Japan are working on the Global Combat Air Programme (GCAP) which merges the UK-led British Aerospace (BAE) Systems 'Tempest' with Japan's 'Mitsubishi F-X', while France, Germany and Spain are working on the Système de combat aérien du futur (SCAF). Even nations that enjoy sovereignty over the design cycle of complex platforms do outsource some sub-systems to Tier II/Tier III vendors in different geographies around the globe for commercial considerations. The lessons for India are that in complex programmes it will have to work in collaboration with like-minded nations. India has had some experience of this in terms of BrahMos and the HF-24 Marut in the past. We need to share the R&D responsibilities and costs.

India must also consider creating cross-dependencies in its supply chain so that India is seen as an equal partner and not just a recipient of a product/technology. For example, resilient microchip supply chains are essential for winning wars. On top of that, India needs to build a resilient, domestic vendor base for items of mass use like ammunition for war endurance as well as to meet its surge capacity.

The current and looming uncertainty in global geo-politics is forcing most nations to de-risk their supply chains from certain geographies if not completely decouple and delinking them. Some global companies including arms manufacturers are keen to establish their businesses in India not only to meet the need for sustenance of existing inventories of their platforms in service in the Indian armed forces but to also meet the demands of their other customers located worldwide. Such initiatives lead to an overlap between civil and military needs like in the case of servicing of CFM and Leading Edge Aviation Propulsion (LEAP) aero engines of Safran and GE. There may be a need to encourage such activities through policy reforms ranging from fiscal to provisioning of land in defence industrial corridors, FDI and licensing, among others.

Aim

This Chapter aims to highlight various reforms being initiated by the government to encourage domestic manufacturing of military hardware by Indian companies, startups and entrepreneurs independently or in the form of joint ventures (JVs) with defence PSUs or foreign vendors and by foreign OEMs directly to meet the needs of a global market or Indian armed forces.

Indigenisation and Innovation

India's armed forces have a large inventory of imported platforms ranging from ICVs (BMP), tanks (T-72, T-90), AD systems (Schilka, Strela, Igla etc), aircraft (Su-30, MiG-29, Mirage 2000, Rafale, Hawk etc), helicopters (Mi-17, Apache, Chinook, Sea King and Kamov) and ships/submarines (EKM877, Scorpene). The serviceability state of these systems defines their operational readiness. This is directly dependent upon our ability to either maintain, repair or service them in India independently or with the help of foreign OEMs. The cost of maintaining equipment throughout its life cycle is a costly enterprise. The effort for sustenance of existing platforms of foreign origin through the indigenisation of spares and accessories is hence important. Its subset also includes the indigenisation of subsystems (communication, combat management systems, IFF, fire control systems) and weapon systems development which also need to be upgraded independently or with the help of the OEM. The overall aim of such indigenisation is 'import substitution' cutting down costs of maintenance and ultimately reducing foreign dependency.

Innovation on the other hand is the development of new capabilities, systems and platforms from R&D to manufacturing. It calls for a different approach and mindset. It will involve defining a 'problem statement' and seeking solutions from the industry, academia, R&D establishments and entrepreneurs. India has one of the largest talent pools of professors, teachers and students as part of our technical institutes. The talent pool has to be harnessed (and even a small percentage can make a difference). Innovation is fundamentally the designing of a new product and can range from small platforms (drones, ammunition, software, communication and cryptography etc) which can be pursued by MSMEs and startups to complex platforms (light tanks, ATAGS, bridges) under Make I and Make II by larger defence manufacturers independently or in partnership with foreign OEMs under the Strategic Partnership model. The range of reforms undertaken by the MoD addresses both indigenisation and innovation aspects.

MoD: Policy Framer

The first and one of the most important policy changes in the field of encouraging Atmanirbharta in defence is an increase in FDI limits. The government has announced FDI of up to 74 per cent through the automatic route and beyond 74 per cent through the government route on a case-to-case basis. The latter will help a foreign OEM to establish a 100 per cent owned subsidiary in India. It will accelerate the establishment of MRO facilities for foreign platforms and is poised to be a game-changer.

Defence Industry Corridors (DICs) offer a major opportunity to boost our defence manufacturing capability. The way these DICs shape up in the future will define our overall defence industry ecosystem. As of date, two DICs have already been established in Uttar Pradesh and Tamil Nadu with several sub-nodes. The purpose of establishing these DICs is to catalyse and spur indigenous defence manufacturing to propel forward the overall vision of consolidation and expansion of India's Military Industrial Complex (MIC). The DIC will also provide employment and opportunities for the development of under-developed pockets of the country like Agra, Aligarh, Chitrakoot, Jhansi, Kanpur, Coimbatore, Chennai, Hosur, Salem etc. Currently, there may be a need to examine the feasibility of establishing additional domain-centric DICs based on the operational requirements of the Armed forces, capitalising on the already existing defence R&D and production ecosystem prevailing in some parts of the country. Clusterisation of DIC industries for avionics, heavy and bulky terrestrial platforms, small arms, ammunition and explosives will introduce efficiency and cut down costs. The DIC of border states must cater for MRO of equipment to reduce turnaround times.

The revision of the Defence Acquisition Procedure (DAP-2020) has been one of the most important changes bringing about conceptual, structural and procedural reforms in the acquisition procedure of capital equipment by the Armed Forces. The DAP-2020 prioritises the acquisition of Indigenous Designed, Developed and Manufactured (IDDM) products. It also offers simplified procedures for the acquisition of products and technologies, developed under the Innovations for Defence Excellence (iDEX) and Make-II routes. Under the Make category with government funding (Make I), the services are actively pursuing 149 projects through co-development with the Indian defence industry, including MSMEs and defence start-ups.

The shift underway in capital procurements is revelatory in the emphasis on domestic procurements. There has also been an improvement in the capital domestic procurement in FY 2021-22 (an approximate increase of 64.5 per cent) and FY 2022-23 (an approximate increase of 68 per cent). To give a boost to India's defence manufacturing industry, 75 per cent of the total procurement budget for FY 2023-24 has been set aside for domestic defence manufacturers. On the revenue side, the Defence Procurement Manual (DPM), which deals with procurement for sustenance requirements, has been revised and is in the final stages of approval. To promote indigenisation, a separate chapter on 'promoting self-reliance through Innovation and Indigenisation' is proposed to be added to the revised DPM-24.

Manufacturing of arms, ammunition, and explosives since independence was the sole preserve of ordnance factories and Defence Public Sector Undertakings (DPSUs). Opening the sectors to Indian private industry has been a major achievement. This has been achieved through the simplification of the defence licensing procedure and the rationalisation of the Defence Product List. The government has also exempted licensing of those parts and components that have already been de-licensed by increasing the validity period of the license from three to 15 years. The provision of a level playing field to the private industry is a work in progress.

The DMA has come out with five Positive Indigenisation Lists (PILs) in consultation with the services listing 509 items that are prioritised to be developed/manufactured in India. This is a major initiative of the government. It helps the defence industry to make long-term investments and capability-building in areas of their expertise and choosing. Out of these 509 items, 98 projects worth Rs 1,53,993 crores have already been contracted, which has given a major boost to the Indian defence industry. While the PILs aim to manufacture bigger platforms indigenously, simultaneously there is a drive for the identification and indigenisation of high-value complex spare parts through the domestic defence industry. An online portal 'Srijan' has been created towards this end.

Some future initiatives that are under consideration are as follows:

- Policy framework for Industry-led Defence R&D ecosystem leveraging the PPP structure.
- Reforming Testing, Trials and Certification protocols with a thrust on self-certification.

- National mission for the development of critical systems and technologies such as aero-engines, sensors, and critical/strategic materials.
- Reforms and restructuring of DPSUs.

Indian Military: The User

The process of indigenisation can succeed only if services take ownership of the initiative. This will require a major mindset change. As brought out earlier, the two conflicts have reinforced the concept of Atmanirbharta and the services are now fully part of the program. The services have identified and created a roadmap for indigenisation of selected weapons (Tanks and BMPs), ammunition and radars spelling out a time-bound action plan to achieve 100 per cent indigenisation. The three services have undertaken internal reforms to promote the cause of indigenisation and innovation.

- ***Army.*** The Indian Army has established the Army Design Bureau (ADB) for innovation. It has put out problem statements for academics and entrepreneurs. These statements are part of iDEX. For indigenisation, it has opened the Defence Indigenisation Cell (DIC) under the Master General Ordnance (MGO). This cell closely interacts with the Base Workshops and the Base Repair Depots (BRDs) as well as all other stakeholders for the indigenisation of spares including hand-holding wherever needed.
- ***Navy.*** The Indian Navy's Weapons and Electronic Systems Engineering Establishment (WESEE) is a premier systems integration centre that has played a pivotal role in seamlessly integrating a diverse array of weapons, sensors, and electronic systems into a variety of naval platforms, including surface ships, submarines, aircraft, and aircraft carriers. WESEE's expertise ensures the cohesive operation and optimal performance of complex systems, enhancing the combat capabilities and overall effectiveness of the Indian naval fleet. For indigenisation, the Navy is also looking to utilise its Directorate of Indigenisation to complement the WESEE.

- ***Indian Air Force.*** The Indian Air Force (IAF) has an in-house Software Development Institute (SDI) at Bengaluru which develops mission planning and debrief systems for all types of aircraft, especially in the field of avionics software systems and integration. The IAF complements this effort through the Directorate of Indigenisation cell.

A Defence Indigenisation Committee has also been set up under Secretary DMA to review the progress on indigenisation and grant exemption for the import of spares, ammunition etc for maintenance of the existing fleet. The committee has been able to draw out a roadmap for the indigenisation of major spares and assemblies that are currently being imported for the upkeep of the existing inventory.

Defence R&D: The Catalyst

To provide impetus to Indigenous defence R&D and push the envelope on technological innovation and indigenisation, a Technology Development Fund (TDF) has been set up. This is managed jointly by DRDO and Invest India. It is a grant-in-aid scheme with the stated aim of defence innovation and indigenisation. An increased limit of Rs 50 crores (from Rs 10 crores earlier) has brought in newer and bigger opportunities. Also, 25 per cent of the defence R&D budget has been earmarked for the private sector.

To further the defence innovation ecosystem, the Indian government started the iDEX program to create an ecosystem to foster innovation and technology development in defence and aerospace by engaging start-ups, MSMEs, individual innovators, R&D institutes and academia. Since the launch of iDEX during DefExpo in 2018, a total of 440 challenges have been released by user directorates and branches in the form of problem definition statements, out of which 316 projects have been accepted by the services. Under the iDEX program, it is planned not only to develop at least 100 niche technology products but also their induction into the services. The success of iDEX schemes led to iDEX Prime and now ADITI (Acing Development of Innovating Technologies with iDEX), which aims to provide up to Rs 25 crores to startups for defence-related R&D and innovation.

The huge talent pool of Indian academia has also been roped in to provide the necessary foundational S&T required for boosting innovation. Incubation centres have been established at major educational institutes across the country by DRDO. Their role is to provide the necessary structural and institutional support for the ideas and innovations of students to progress from the concept to the prototype stage. In some cases, services are also collaborating with IITs to resolve immediate problems of a technical nature.

Defence Manufacturing: The Outcome

Improvements in the defence manufacturing sector started with the long overdue corporatisation of the Ordnance Factory Boards (OFB). Established in 1801, OFB is one of the oldest and largest defence production organisations globally with 41 factories across India. In 2021, the production units of OFB were converted into seven DPSUs. It was also decided that the new OFBs will receive government support only till 2026-27. This will assist in creating a level playing field with the Private Industry. The decision to corporatise OFB stems from the government's intent to streamline operations, increase accountability and foster innovation in defence production since the OFB plays a crucial role in meeting the Indian Armed Forces' ammunition and equipment requirements. By transitioning to a corporate structure, OFB has started to leverage private-sector expertise, enhancing competitiveness and aligning itself with global best practices in manufacturing.

Within the country, the bulk of defence production, up to 80 per cent, is undertaken by DPSUs. The contributing share of private industry towards the defence manufacturing ecosystem is approximately 20 per cent. To enhance defence manufacturing and to align our defence industry with international standards, there is a need to invigorate private industry towards excellence in defence manufacturing. Therefore, the scope of widening our defence manufacturing base from public to private companies needs to be seen not only from the perspective of self-reliance but also in India becoming a net exporter of defence equipment, sub-assemblies, spares and associated services.

The Defence Production and Exports Promotion Policy (DPEPP-2020) targets a turnover of US$ 25 billion, including exports of US$ 5 billion by 2025 making India a net exporter instead of the net importer. With Indian defence exports jumping by more than 10 times (from Rs 1522 crores in 2016-17 to Rs 15918 crores in 2022-23), India has entered the list of global exporters. India is presently exporting defence equipment to more than 100 nations and the intention is to achieve domestic defence production worth Rs 1,75,000 crores and defence exports worth Rs 35,000 crores by 2024-25.

Some of the notable achievements of DPSUs include indigenously built INS Vikrant, Tejas multirole fighter aircraft, Akash surface-to-air missile system, Arjun Main Battle Tank and so on. On the other hand, the Private Defence Industry in collaboration with DRDO/DPSU or Foreign OEMs has been able to produce Pinaka MBRLs, K9 Vajras, ATAGS, C-295 transport aircraft, Brahmos, Floating Dock for the Navy (FDN11), Offshore Patrol Vessels and Interceptor boats for the Coast Guards. To bolster self-reliance, DRDO, DPSUs, MSMEs and the private industry are being encouraged to enter into JVs/SPVs with foreign OEMs for the manufacture of defence equipment in India. For example, Airbus Defence and Space has partnered with Tata Advanced Systems Ltd (TASL) for the acquisition and manufacture of 56 Airbus C-295 aircraft. Similarly, Reliance Defence Ltd has JVs with Dassault Aviation, France for the assembly of large aerostructures for Falcon and Rafale engine doors and with Thales for full integration facility for AESA Radar, Spectra EW suite and maintenance support for Front Section Optronics (FSO) for Rafale aircraft. HAL and Safran Aircraft Engines are also collaborating in developing aero engines for helicopters.

Prognosis and Way Forward

Defence Acquisition Procedure (DAP 2020) derives its ethos and spirit from the clarion call of an 'Atmanirbhar Bharat' and 'Make in India'. While it is true that DAP 2020 has provided much-needed impetus to the indigenisation of the defence sector, it also cannot be denied that there is some scope for further improvement. A key issue is the relatively long processing time for the completion of projects and some delays in obtaining financial clearances. There are some projects which may require some additional time to complete. These create challenges in the provisioning of capabilities to the services at the optimal time and need to be further fine-tuned. The current provisions need to be amended to encourage the participation of MSMEs and small industries in the indigenisation efforts.

The Gross Expenditure on R&D (GERD) in India has doubled from 2010-11 to 2020-21. However, India's GERD as a percentage of GDP has remained well below 1 per cent since 1990. Most developed countries spend more than 2 per cent of their GDP on R&D, eg US (3 per cent), and China (2.4 per cent). India's spending on defence R&D requires a major boost. A strong ecosystem for enabling R&D, combined with a manufacturing strength that rapidly converts experimental prototypes into military products at scale, is a strategic necessity. Hence, adequate funding needs to be given to defence research.

DRDO is the premier defence R&D entity. However, considering the capabilities and capacities developed by the private defence industry, a need exists to encourage and involve private industry in defence R&D. DRDO should focus only on niche technologies, security-sensitive projects and complex systems, which are difficult to address by private players. R&D for contemporary technologies should be left, rather reserved, for the private sector. DRDO also requires a re-orientation/revitalisation through introspection.

Retention of talent, scientists and Subject Matter Experts (SMEs) is paramount for defence innovation and indigenisation. The defence manufacturing and R&D ecosystem of the US is based on proactive engagement to recruit, retain and cultivate talent by offering financial support and various incentives. China also has various incentive programmes such as Thousand Talent Plan (TTP), Talent 11, Talent 1000, Talent 10000 initiatives etc. We need to proactively identify and vigorously implement incentive programs and attractive schemes to retain existing talent and encourage reverse migration.

The Indian defence sector is in its evolutionary phase during which it would require significant handholding to make it globally competitive on price and quality indices. Easy access to state-of-the-art testing infrastructure is imperative for the organic growth of the design and development ecosystem, ensuring safety, reliability and intended use. The Indian government has opened up test labs and proof ranges/field firing ranges spread across the country for use by the private industry. However, an independent umbrella agency needs to be established to facilitate the testing and certification of defence-related products as per international standards. This infrastructure can be set up through the Defence Testing Infrastructure Scheme (DTIS). The Quality Assurance processes also need to be reformed so they are non-intrusive, prevention-based and free from Inspector influence. The policies must also be modified to cater for the significant number of commercial components (non-military grade) inside modern platforms.

The MRO upgrade and other lifecycle support activities constitute a major part towards the sustenance of the Armed Forces and are often more cost-intensive than the initial capital investment. There is a substantially large amount of revenue available to the Indian defence industry, if MRO work is performed within the country. With appropriate incentives, private industry can also play a crucial role in set-up up such facilities in DICs through JVs/ToT with DPSUs/foreign OEMs, wherever deemed necessary by the service HQ. This would not only enable MRO of defence equipment of our Armed Forces but also facilitate India in becoming the 'MRO Hub for the world' in the long run.

The lack of a level playing field between the private and public sector companies has remained a persistent demand of in the Private defence industry. These relate to certain provisions which may be perceived to be favouring the DPSUs over the private sector. A holistic consideration to address all such issues and provide a level playing field to the private sector to make them equal partners in the design, development and manufacturing of military equipment is under deliberation at appropriate levels.

Conclusion

'Atmanirbharta in Defence' is not only a matter of strategic necessity but also a significant driver of economic growth, technological advancement and national security. It represents a pathway towards self-reliance, which is crucial for our nation as it strives for economic growth and strategic independence. Threats from adversaries leave India with no other option but to augment its defence capabilities to secure its national security interests. As we walk along the path of 'Atmanirbharta in Defence', all stakeholders involved in indigenisation efforts, public or private, need to align with the concept of 'Achieving capability to fight future wars with completely Indian solutions.

India became the fifth largest economy in the world in 2023 when its GDP in PPP terms crossed that of the UK. As India marches towards realising the dream of a 'New India', it not only remains committed to peace and stability across the world but also believes that strategic autonomy, issue-based partnerships with like-minded partners and indigenous defence capabilities are the foundations to enduring peace. A strong and prosperous India will have the capability and capacity to act as the anchor for regional and even global stability in the long run. A strong and resilient R&D capability combined with a robust indigenous defence manufacturing infrastructure is a strategic necessity in the context of the increasingly volatile, regional and global geo-political environment. A series of events in the past few years has exposed the vulnerability of global supply chains reinforcing India's belief in building indigenous capabilities and capacities. There is a growing realisation to find Indian solutions to our unique challenges. The 'Indian Way' is the order of the day.

13

Transformation and Management of Change

> "*The change in the mindscape will lead to the changes in the landscape.*"
>
> —Author

Change is the unwritten law of nature – "परिवर्तन ही प्रकृति का नियम है". These profound and perennial words of wisdom are part of Lord Krishna's teachings in Srimad Bhagwat Gita. The 'inevitability of change' finds mention in many other ancient philosophical works also. Heraclitus, a Greek philosopher had said that 'change is the only constant in life'. Indeed, everything in this world is transitional and subject to change.

Change is also associated with survival. Charles Darwin in his famous work 'Origins of the Species' stated that 'variation, inheritance, selection, timing and adaptation' are important for any species to survive. The process of 'natural selection' embodies the principle that only the fittest will survive. Subsequent naturalists cum scientists like Richard Dawkins further expanded on this concept and said that the ultimate beneficiary of selection is the gene which passes the best traits to the successor generation. Be that as it may, the main import of all these thinkers is that only those behaviours and attributes which are adaptive, transformative, ruggedised and honed enough through time, experience and interaction with the external environment have better chances of survival. Like organisms, organisations too need to change to survive. This is especially true for structured and hierarchical organisations like that of the armed forces. The environment in which organisations operate is never static. It is evolving constantly with new threats, challenges, players, technologies, dimensions and methodologies. Hence change is important.

Nature of Change

Changes are of two types. These are either gradual or disruptive. Gradual change is incremental with the process of change occurring over some time. In nature, it gives time to the 'species' to adapt to the changing environment. On the other hand, a disruptive change occurs when the operating environment changes in an unforeseen manner like the coming of the Ice Age that wiped out the dinosaurs. Organisations need to prepare for both types of changes.

The adaptations and changes incorporated by the Indian Armed Forces to meet the advancement in warfare and the emerging threat envelope are good examples of gradual change. After the 1962 war, the Army introduced mountain divisions. The lessons of the 1971 war and the need for mobility and deeper strikes saw the creation of RAPID Divisions. Doctrinal changes like Cold Start or Proactive Strategy and interchanging roles between Pivot Formations and Strike Formations were the result of Operation Parakram. Similarly, the 'Dynamic Response Strategy' was born out of the experience of Balakot air strikes and Operation Zafran. The Integrated Battle Group (IBG) models, under debate nowadays, were a product of the Dynamic Response Strategy, which is based on preemption and proactive operations. The Indian Air Force too introduced new doctrines and concepts with the induction of the next generation of fighter aircraft. The introduction of 4th and 4.5-generation multirole fighter aircraft has led to a change in thinking from a favourable air situation to air superiority/dominance and air supremacy. The concept of air defence has also changed from base to area defence. The IAF also adapted to bring in timely changes such as the Air Battle Management of Composite Offensive Air Package (COAP). The Indian Navy also graduated from a brown water to a blue water navy and the need for a responsive force has brought in concepts like Mission Deployment.

A disruptive change occurs over a lesser time horizon. It requires a transformative approach rather than an adaptive one to survive. The disruptive changes in the industry occur largely due to changes in technology or due to a policy change that is beyond the control of the industry. The story of Kodak, a leading camera maker using photographic films, when faced with the disruptive digital camera technology was slow to adopt and largely non-responsive. This is often quoted in management circles as the reason for the change in its fortunes and eventual downfall. The Remington typewriter company faced a similar fate with the advent of computers and printers. These organisations, like the dinosaurs, were not prepared for the sudden change in the operating environment that led to their extinction.

I believe that the prospects of an Ice Age are looming large before us. Global geo-politics is in a state of flux presenting unprecedented security challenges. The global economy is still recovering from the aftereffects of Covid-19 and disruption in food and energy supply chains, while disruptive technology is affecting businesses from manufacturing to marketing. Some critical technologies are also affecting the character of war and the method of warfighting. The armed forces will have to be prepared to meet the challenges caused largely due to the flux in global geo-politics, fluctuations in the global geo-economics and flurry of technological changes. For tradition-bound organisations like the armed forces, this will test the limits of their ingenuity and imagination.

Threats, Challenges and Opportunities

Unlike organisms, most organisations are intelligent enough to foresee change. They constantly evaluate the operating environment, and current threats and attempt to predict future challenges so that they can be preemptive and proactive in their strategies to adapt and even transform.

In the armed forces, most of our planning is based on meeting threats and challenges. A threat is imminent, easy to identify and requires immediate action to counter it. Challenges are also as easily identifiable as threats but have a larger gestation period of manifestation. The second and third-order effects and long-term consequences of threats are slightly more difficult to identify. Armed forces are organised to meet future threats and challenges as and when they present themselves. Opportunities are relatively difficult to predict and those organisations that are adaptive enough to exploit opportunities will be more successful in the future than those which are merely preparing to meet the threats and challenges. Crystal gazing about the future is hence emerging as a science in which many organisations invest substantially. Net assessment and simulation are other names for such forecasting.

Forecasting and Prediction

Forecasting the future is, however, a difficult enterprise, even for those equipped with reams of data and information about known and unknown variables. Despite this, crystal gazing for the future is an important exercise, as it prepares an organisation for meeting threats and exploiting opportunities over a longer time horizon. It exercises the collective intellect concerning the broad spectrum of challenges, affording it the necessary time for resources, reallocation, inter-se prioritisation and organisational restructuring.

Most forecasting is based on linear modelling. It relies on past data and trends to predict the likely future outcomes. Demographics is an example of linear modelling where population statistics like the growth rate, mean age of the population, gender distribution etc can be predicted. Similarly, climate change is another area where linear modelling can be used to predict issues like an increase in global temperature, rise in sea levels or melting of polar and continental ice caps. Climate-induced changes in cropping patterns could be secondary outcomes of such predictions, though prediction patterns in climate change combine both linear and non-linear methods with the former dominating in the short-term and the latter in the medium to long term.

The occurrence of geo-political events, geo-economic development and technological changes are difficult to predict as they do not follow a linear path. It may be easy to make a reasonable assessment of the growth of CNP of nation-states or the emerging contours of strategic competition between potential adversaries but the actual trigger for a conflict will always be different from the anticipated 'wild cards' to disrupt linear modelling-based predictions. Political pundits are hence always evaluating issues like 'why nations fail' or trying to find a common thread that connects the 'rise and fall' of great powers. Analysis of the state of the economy based on consumption patterns, industrial outputs, social/skill development and many such factors results in the prediction of GDP growth rates. Yet, the linear modelling of economic activity can be disrupted by pandemics and wars which are difficult to predict. Some technologies like computation or communication witness geometrical progression or take the form of an 'S' shape curve in their manifestation and market exploitation. Disruptive technologies like AI/ML or even platforms like drones can upset many established processes and stable ecosystems. Discovery of a new technology, however, creates an upheaval and major disruptions in the existing paradigm. It affects many fields like social behaviour, economy, industry, governance and of course the military.

The current geo-political events in Europe and the wider Middle East have induced uncertainty and instability in the global and regional security environment. The capability building of armed forces is dependent upon financial outlays which are in turn dependent on the overall economic performance of the nation. However, changes in manufacturing or supply chain disruptions can affect military preparedness. These two issues are insignificant in comparison to the changes being induced due to technology disruptions.

Armed Forces and Change

Warfare is currently at the threshold of a major revolution. The first revolution in military affairs (RMA) of manoeuvre warfare is gradually yielding space to the second RMA of net-centric operations. Newer technologies in the fields of AI, ML, data analytics, cryptography, and quantum computing on one hand and stealth, drones, hypersonics and long-range precision targeting on the other are poised to usher in a new revolution of convergence. The Indian armed forces have been trying to catch up to the first and second RMA and were always following the change. They now need to lead the change and attempt to enter the emerging RMA along with advanced militaries if not before them.

To usher in such a change, the process for reforms will range from organisational, structural, and conceptual to doctrinal and cultural. It will require a fresh approach to our thought process. The change in the mindscape will lead to changes in the landscape. Being innovative, inventive, imaginative and ingenious will be the new mantra to remain ahead of the transformation (learning) curve.

The establishment of Joint/Integrated Theatre Commands (ITCs) is one such reform that will form the bedrock on which the future set of reforms will be undertaken. The establishment of ITCs will separate 'Force Generation' activity from 'Force Application' in other words, operational activity will be handled by one set of commanders and officers, whereas the raise, train and sustain functions will be overseen by a different set of commanders and officers. It will bring in efficiency in both processes, providing impetus to fresh thinking and nurturing the spirit of experimentation to meet emerging challenges and exploit fleeting opportunities. Some of the futuristic trends that will be aided by the creation of ITCs are as follows:

- Move from Single Domain to Multi-Domain Operations.
- Fusing of the space and cyber domain with the traditional domains of warfare.
- Digitisation of battlefield information, visualisation and control.
- Graduate from net-centric to data-centric warfighting.
- Promote the next level of integration.
- Trigger organisational reforms at lower echelons.
- Expand warfare into the cognitive domain.
- Provide flexibility (mental and organisational) to futuristic warfighting.

Change Management

Organisations, especially hierarchical and tradition-bound, as brought out earlier, are status-quoist by nature. They follow Newton's first law of motion on preferring to 'remain in a steady-state of uniform motion or rest unless an external force is applied'. When faced with the prospects of change, people and organisations consider what they will lose 'individually' rather than thinking what they will gain 'collectively'. The status-quoist attitude of such organisations can only be changed by applying Newton's second law of motion which states that the 'rate of change of momentum of a body is directly proportional to the external force' applied and the direction of movement is also dependent on the direction of force. Organisations also follow the third law of motion of creating a reaction equal to the force applied. Hence change management has to be a healthy mix of scientific and management principles. Some of the principles that help bring about the change in mindset are discussed below:

- ***Guiding Coalition.*** To bring about transformative change, there is a need to set up a 'guiding coalition' that will think through the process of reforms and then guide the echelons at lower levels of management. In the armed forces, this is best done through a top-down approach – the COSC comprising the top leadership was the guiding coalition to think and guide the reform process. The coalition then develops a vision and strategy, clearly outlining the desired future state. We called this experiment – COSC's strategic discussion – Operation. Tiranga. The message that the four seniormost people were working together was a powerful one.
- ***Role and Goal Clarity.*** There are three separate apex organisations headed by the CDS, COSC, HQ IDS and DMA. The clear definition of roles and responsibilities of these three roles and the interlinkages of HQ IDS with service HQ to bring about this change were important. The decisions of COSC were to be implemented by HQ IDS in conjunction with service HQ. DMA was to keep the office of Hon'ble RM informed. Once the

contours of the creation of ITC were clear, it was DMA's responsibility to get the approval of CCS.

- ***Vision.*** Mapping the route of transformation from the beginning to the end and encapsulating it as a 'vision' was important. Unless the vision becomes clear to stakeholders, they are unlikely to support the change. It's imperative to communicate the changed vision relentlessly, ensuring widespread understanding and buy-in. Leaders must empower broad-based action by removing obstacles and encouraging initiatives.
- ***Creating a Sense of Urgency.*** This was done by presenting a bigger challenge of enforced reform if not done internally. It compels people to act with passion and purpose and creates momentum for them to achieve the vision themselves. This sense of urgency can be reinforced through several factors such as talks (an impending Ice Age), apprehension (change in government may lead to a change in direction or momentum) and awareness.
- ***Dissemination.*** There was a need to take the message of reforms to the rank and file. The reforms being attempted would have impacted the middle-level officers the maximum. They would be involved in carrying forward the reforms in the balance of their service life. The outreach involved travelling to all Commands, involving all tri-services institutes/commands/agencies and sub-committees of the COSC in becoming part of this movement.
- ***Short-term Gains.*** There is a necessity to showcase gains to the members of the audience. The initial efforts towards integration were showcased and advertised to drive home the message that reforms will be crucial for inculcating an embodied culture of jointness. It was also emphasised that jointness and integration will take time and there will be ups and downs in the process. Generating short-term wins such as initial integration and jointness initiatives builds momentum and reinforces the change effort. The process continues by consolidating gains, producing

more changes and progressively embedding these changes into the organisational fabric. Ultimately, this leads to a new culture of change with the new approaches firmly anchored within the organisation.

The creation of ITCs is one of the most transformative reforms being attempted within the Indian armed forces since independence. The separation of 'Force Application' and 'Force Generation' will redistribute the existing power structure/equilibrium. Naturally, there will be resistance to such a change. The process of organisational restructuring was based on the edifice of jointness and integration. A three-stage process was evolved with all stages being attempted simultaneously.

- ***Jointness.*** Jointness is essentially a mindset and its effectiveness, being psychological, is difficult to measure. Despite three distinct Service Specific Cultures, even in joint service organisations, officers carry their service identities. Therefore, creating a 'Joint Culture' is essential for establishing Joint Operational Structures and ensuring the success of joint organisations and commands. The Joint Culture must respect the uniqueness of each service while promoting original thinking, seamless sharing of knowledge, and the adoption of innovative, inventive, imaginative, and indigenous approaches. It should encourage receptivity to divergent ideas, prioritise the message over the messenger and establish non-hierarchical structures to reduce delays in staff work. Symbology and rituals, such as flags, badges and commemorative events are vital for fostering a sense of belonging and speeding up the adoption of Joint Culture.
- ***Integration.*** Integration is the merging of diverse entities or organisations. It is a visible and measurable activity combining the unique capabilities of each service to enhance war-fighting efficiency and system effectiveness. While optimisation of resources such as manpower, infrastructure and time is a byproduct, it is not the primary goal of integration. Integration is essential for creating ITCs and it acts as a bridge between the

abstract philosophy of Jointness and the establishment of ITCs. Key areas for integration include communications, operations, intelligence, training, logistics, HR, legal, administration and maintenance. Integration 2.0 emphasises the issuance of Joint Instructions, Joint Orders and Joint Policy Directives, thereby formalising integration efforts through a consultative process.

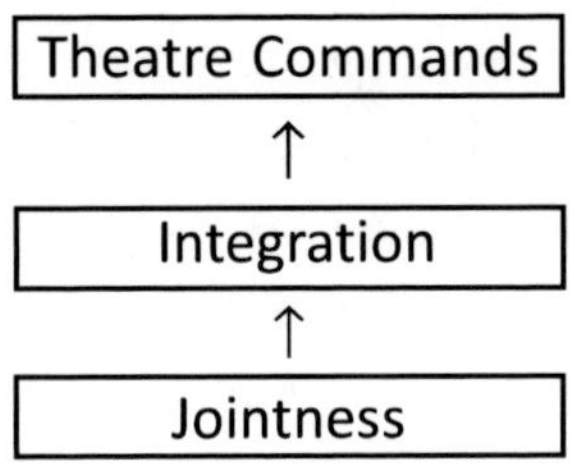

Figure 2: 3-Stage Process for Establishment of Theatre Commands.

Lessons

The journey to the creation of ITCs has just begun. One of the purposes of this article is to disseminate to the stakeholders the scope of what is being attempted, the route being followed and the expected gains. ITC is not the end state but the beginning of another set of reforms. There are lessons that one has learnt in this 18-month journey period while building consensus and disseminating the message of reforms to the officers of the three services. Some of the important ones are as follows:

- ***Patience.*** One needs to inculcate patience as changes will take time to percolate down to the soldier, airman and sailor level. There needs to be a recognition that ideas for jointness and integration can be found anywhere and at any rank. One must listen to the idea, develop it, discuss it and disseminate it for implementation. This can only happen by meeting and listening to individuals from all ranks and services.
- ***Take People Along.*** There needs to be a concerted attempt to take people along the path to transformation. Everyone involved in this exercise from the decision-making to the implementation

organisations must be made to feel that they are part of the process.

- ***Listen.*** This is a big virtue. When change is being attempted, everyone will have an idea – his/her idea of change. There is a need to listen and absorb the message from all sections of the stakeholders. It needs to be remembered that 'What is being said is more important than who is saying it'.
- ***Symbology.*** Symbology is important for jointness and jointmanship. It will reinforce faith in jointness and integration. The purple colour needs to be internalised, normalised and standardised across the three services. This will happen through cross-staffing, parades and movies. Theaterisation will be the outcome of cross-spectrum consensus, both internally and externally. These include promoting a joint culture which retains the best of the three services, something akin to the highest common factor (HCF) rather than the bare minimum or the lowest common denominator (LCD). This joint culture must promote professionalism in the form of dissent and competence.
- ***Point of No Return.*** In transformative change management, the point of no return refers to a critical juncture in the change process where going back to the old way of doing things becomes significantly difficult, expensive, or even impossible. It's a tipping point where the organisation has become too invested in the transformation to realistically abandon it.

Conclusion

The journey to bring about change in organisations having a strong culture and tracking of their own is difficult. The propensity of the people to adopt a new faith of jointness and practice of Joint Culture was not easy. Managing change becomes easy once people realise the perpetual and eternal nature of change.

In Hindu mythology, the trinity of Gods is responsible for creation, preservation and destruction. The three are seen as part of a continuous cycle. The armed forces too need to follow the cyclical process to evolve or reincarnate. While creation and preservation are easy, the destruction and discarding of the old is a challenge. In management parlance, there is a term 'creative destruction'. One has to be imaginative to discard, dispose, demolish and destroy the old. It is a creative function and not a destructive one.

Section D

IMPORTANT TALKS

14

Global Futures 2035: Future Security Challenges

Synergia Foundation International Conclave

18 Nov 23

Allow me to begin with a quote from HG Wells, whom I consider as the original futurologist:

> "The past is the beginning of a beginning, and all that is and has been, is but the twilight of the dawn".

Trying to know what the future holds for us has been one of the oldest obsessions of the human mind. Most of us have grown up reading HG Wells, Jules Verne and Aldous Huxley. Some of their predictions for the future like nuclear weapons, Aircraft, Tanks and Submarines have come true while others like Martian Invasion or Time Machine have not. Predicting the future accurately, therefore, is not easy.

In India, Vedic Astrology to a large extent was driven by the motivation to visualise or predict the future. The future is motivated by change. We all have to adapt to change and adopt it, lest we are subjected to what another futurologist Alvin Toffler prophesied as 'Future Shocks'. Over the past few years, the pace of change has gathered exponential momentum. It is increasing in geometric proportions, and outpacing the present and the past to bring the future to our doorsteps, rather prematurely.

Some aspects of the future are easier to forecast. Their prediction is based on a study of past data, examination of existing patterns and scientific modelling. Demographics is one such area where the ageing of the population in developed countries and imbalance in population growth will lead to a shift in economic activity, migration and urbanisation. All three factors will contribute to inter and intra-state tensions in the future. Climate change is another area where issues like a rise in global temperature, extreme weather, rise in sea levels and melting of polar ice caps may induce changes in cropping patterns leading to food and water scarcity. Advances in technology and economic growth also, by and large, follow a linear progression. Both have the potential to alter existing power equations.

Inter-state relations are difficult to predict. They do not follow a linear progression and are influenced by unforeseen events or 'Wild Cards'. As far as the business of conflict is concerned, both geo-politics and conflict have more than a casual connection.

In my view future security challenges will be driven by two things – The trajectory of the ongoing unprecedented nature of changes in global geo-politics and Technology that is changing the nature and character of conflict.

Changes induced by geo-political developments or those ushered in by technology have two things in common – both induce behavioural changes i.e. geo-politics in the behaviour of a nation-state, whereas technology affects social behaviours commencing at the individual level. World order, as the name suggests is designed to maintain global peace. However, geo-political competition may induce tension and conflict. Technology introduces new ways to retain military edge over adversaries during such conflicts.

Geo-Political Changes

The interplay of geography, political power and strategic considerations interact to shape the behaviour of nation-states. Geo-political events also have the potential to shape national ideologies and influence their ideological narratives. Geo-political events also affect Geo-economies. The current flux in the global geo-economical order can be attributed directly to the Volatile, Uncertain, Complex and Ambiguous (VUCA) environment ushered by what can be called a 'Global Disorder'. Old rules and maxims of diplomacy are fading away, new ones are emerging, and events are unfolding at a speed and pace that exceeds the ability of decision-makers to react effectively.

In an attempt to visualise global futures in 2035, I will take the help of current trends to extrapolate the future with the hope that some of these will act as reference points for further debates during the conclave. I believe that 'Unipolarity' will shortly become an artefact of the past. A multi-polar Global order with polycentric and polyconic competition and cooperation is likely to emerge. In a polycentric world, multiple centres of power exist, each with its interests and capabilities. These centres interact in a web of competition and cooperation, leading to a polyconic global order. Competition arises over resources, influence and strategic advantages, while cooperation is necessitated by global challenges that no single entity can address alone, such as climate change, terrorism and pandemics. The competition may, however, encourage Low-Intensity Conflict & Proxy wars at the bottom of the pyramid.

Nation-states will find security and comfort in newer alliances and partnerships. These will be subject to frequent realignments to meet the real or perceived challenges. The new re-distribution of power has made the world flatter. It has increased the propensity of big powers to take risks and unlike the past, dominant powers do not hesitate to put boots on the ground. There is an increasing proclivity among nations to enter into conflicts to protect perceived national interests. However, in most cases, most big powers have entered into conflicts without a clear end state or exit strategy. Iraq, Afghanistan and Ukraine are examples of it. A prolonged simmering conflict with spikes of violence is another trend that may continue.

In my understanding, the US cannot simultaneously meet its commitment in the Indo-Pacific, Europe and Asia. It accordingly shifted its focus from the Global War on Terror (GWOT) towards the emerging Grey Zone conflict in the Indo-Pacific. This trend will continue and I think is irreversible. There was a growing perception that Inter-state wars are a thing of the past and have been replaced by Intra-state conflicts and civil wars. This has been proved wrong. Inter-state conflicts occur due to existing but latent disputes. Israel-Hamas, Armenian-Azerbaijan, and Russia-Ukraine are only examples of it. It is hence important to manage differences and disputes.

The Israel-Hamas conflict has the potential to polarise the world. It may usher in new geo-political alignments.

The Russia-Ukraine conflict has crossed the second year. The war in Europe and the Middle East has fuelled fresh tensions. It has accentuated levels of uncertainty even among nations that are not directly affected by the conflict. A combination of increased tensions and rising uncertainties has forced nations to review their national security strategies. The trend is evident and uniform from Europe to Asia.

The Global Supply Chains that were yet to recover from the effects of the COVID-19 pandemic are under strain such as Food, Fertiliser, Energy, medical equipment as well as technologies like semiconductors, rare earth and critical minerals. There is also a new demand for military equipment from Ordinary ammunition to high-end systems. The current defence ecosystem is not geared to meet the surge in demand and its supplies.

Further, challenges to national security may not be a result of interstate competition or uncertainty only. Pandemics and bio-threats, cyber threats, transnational terrorism and nuclear threats will continue to bedevil security planners. The pace of geo-political events is outpacing decision-making abilities. By 2035, we may find more geo-political surprises packed in the 12 years than what we witnessed in the past 120 years.

I will now shift focus towards technology which I believe will also play an important role in shaping global futures.

Technology Driven Future

In the tapestry of time, technology emerges as the weaver of our shared future, intricately shaping the landscape of human existence. The seeds of technological disruption sow fields of possibility, birthing new industries and transforming the very fabric of our economic reality. The nexus of communication technologies has dissolved barriers and distance, fostering a global village where ideas traverse across continents in an instant. Our technological endeavours promise a future where healthcare is personalised, education is democratised and renewable energy sources sustain our planet.

Technological advancements are providing nation-states with new options to secure themselves against the challenges that I just spoke about. At the same time, it is also ushering in new ways of combat. Hypersonic missiles, subsonic drones and higher accuracy have increased the lethality as well as complexities of detection and engagement. Multi-domain sensors and communication have provided improved Battlefield Transparency. The virtual domains of Cyber and Space are uncovering the lethal potentiality of non-kinetic options and are causing an overarching effect on the physical domains. Information is being weaponised through targeting of the Cognitive domain.

Technology and Security

Technology is also emerging as the new currency of power. Technology denial regimes existed in the past but now we are witnessing a race to retain technological edge. Technology provides the cutting edge during combat and decides the outcome of conflicts. Advancements in technologies are introducing a new Revolution in Military Affairs (RMA).

A RMA occurs when technology is introduced in large numbers. It forces a change in tactics and concomitantly changes the organisation to support the technology and tactics.

I believe that we are on the cusp of the next RMA which I prefer to call 'Convergence Warfare'. This involves the convergence of the 1st RMA of manoeuvre warfare and the 2nd RMA of Net-Centric Warfare into the current one. It will integrate traditional domains of warfare with emerging domains like cyber and space. New technologies will converge to make the battle space more automated and autonomous where battle space and time will expand and converge at the same time.

The Indian Armed Forces will have to operate in an environment that is rapidly being shaped and reshaped by turns of geo-political events and advancements in technologies. This will require flexibility in our organisational structures as well as our mindsets. We should be ushered in the 3rd RMA along with other nations to remain ahead or at par with the transformation curve.

This will require changes that will range from organisational, structural, doctrinal, and conceptual to behavioural and cultural.

- Our organisational structure must be capable of multi-domain operations (MDO).
- They must be capable of responding seamlessly in the continuum of crisis – confrontation – conflict and combat.
- They must be structured for integrated rapid response through a correct balance between contact and non-contact and kinetic as well as non-kinetic options.
- They must be flexible and adaptive enough to absorb and harness niche, emerging and disruptive technologies.

There is a term used in Management parlance 'Creative Destruction'. It is an oxymoron. It means to create something new, one has to destroy the old. The destruction or discard has to be done in a manner which is creative and helps in the adoption of new processes and technologies. This is the type of change that I visualise will take place shortly. India is also in the Amrit Kaal of its nationhood and the path we take today will decide where we will be in 2047.

Conclusion

To conclude, I would like to recall the Law of Karma as mentioned in Dhammapada.

> "The kind of seed sown will produce that kind of fruit.
>
> Those who do good will reap good results.
>
> Those who do evil will reap evil results."

The global events need to be viewed through this Law based on Cause and Effect. Whatever thoughts and energy you put out, you get back – good or bad. To get what you want, you have to embody and be worthy of those things.

15

Geo-political Impacts of Indo-Pacific Maritime Trade and Connectivity

Indo-Pacific Regional Dialogue 2023

15 Nov 2023

Introduction

Global attention is currently riveted towards the ongoing conflict in Europe and West Asia. These conflicts have caused major disruptions in the global Supply Chains related to Energy, food, fertilisers and defence equipment. They have affected trade, connectivity and the economy of most nations. The worst affected, of course, is the 'Global South' – an unofficial collective of nations which currently lack the resilience and capacities to endure such crises.

Any crisis or conflict in the Indo-Pacific has the potential to cause disruptions on a scale much larger than the ongoing conflicts. India as the fastest growing economy, dependent on the seas/oceans for trade will be affected the maximum.

Historical Connect

India's vision for the Indo-Pacific flows from its historical connection with the region through trade and culture. Hinduism and Buddhism flowed to Southeast Asia in the 1st and 2nd centuries from India, mostly following the maritime routes. The Pallava, Chola, and Srivijaya Empires had close trade and cultural links with countries and ruling dynasties in the Indo-Pacific.

The Indian Mythological legend of Samundra Manthan by Devas (Gods) and Asuras (Demons) in Vishnu Puran is a popular lore in Thailand and Indonesia. Indians worship Varuna, the lord of the seas. Oceans have played an important role in India's mythology and history from ancient times to the present and I believe that oceans will shape its destiny in future.

Geography

Geographically, India has been both a continental power as well as a maritime nation. India's Golden Age, the Gupta Period (3rd-6th Centuries CE), is a testimony to India's combined Continental and Maritime history, character and identity. Land corridors connect India to the Asian landmass – Eastern Europe, West Asia, Central Asia and China. In the 1st century AD, the teachings of Buddha travelled along with trade caravans along the Silk Route. They spread Buddhism to China and Tibet and later to Korea and Japan.

The peninsular shape of India jutting out in the Indian Ocean and island territories in the flanks makes India a natural maritime power. India's pre-dominant geographical position in IOR is further accentuated by the access to IOR being limited by the Chokepoints of Sunda Strait, Lombok Strait, Malacca Straits, Bab-el Mandeb and Mozambique Straits. The current geo-politics and disputed borders have constrained India's continental connectivity. They affect our policies to Act East and Look West.

We are trying to overcome the limitations of geo-politics by trying alternate routes. International North-South Transport Corridor (INSTC), India Middle East Europe Economic Corridor (IMEC), Kaladan Multi-Modal Transit Transport Project, Chabahar Port etc are part of it. On the other hand, the oceans offer us the ability to connect to the world. Economics, trade, expression of cultural and social ties and culture depend on free and open seas. India's destiny lies at the sea.

Indo-Pacific

Historically, the Indo-Pacific is a geographical concept defining a broad expanse of maritime and continental territory of the Pacific and Indian Oceans.

Varying geographical interpretations of the Indo-Pacific, encompass Eastern African and Asian nations, littorals bordering these two Oceans, Australia, New Zealand, Japan, the US and Pacific Island countries. India's viewpoint is best encapsulated in the Words of PM Modi at the Shangri La Dialogue (2018), "India does not see the Indo-Pacific Region as a strategy or as a club of limited members. And by no means do we consider it as directed against any country. A geographical definition, as such, cannot be. India's vision for the Indo-Pacific Region is, therefore, a positive one. It includes all nations in this geography as also others beyond who have a stake in it".

Importance of Indo-Pacific

The importance of the Indo-Pacific Region can be gleaned from the fact that the region encompasses 38 countries, 44 per cent of the global surface area, 65 per cent of the population (58 per cent youth) and 62 per cent of the global GDP. 50 per cent of global trade and 40 per cent of the world's oil passes through these oceans. It has the world's busiest and most strategically significant maritime trade routes which facilitate the movement of goods, energy resources and raw materials between Europe, the Middle East, Africa and Asia. The strategic importance of the region can be gauged from the fact that it contains seven of the ten largest armies in the world and six nuclear powers. It is home to many hot spots such as the 38th parallel, Taiwan, South China Sea and East China Sea disputes, and India-Pakistan & India-China border disputes.

The jostling between global powers in the Indo-Pacific has led to profound power shifts and rebalancing, prompting a reassessment of traditional alignments, forging of new alliances and the emergence of innovative partnerships.

India's Stakes in Indo-Pacific

India's security interests are deeply enmeshed with what happens in the Indo-Pacific. While we are conscious of the security challenges along our Northern and Western borders, we also have a stake in the security of international shipping lanes, as well as in maintaining a free, open, inclusive and rules-based Indo-Pacific.

Most of us are aware that more than 95 per cent of India's trade by volume and 65 per cent by value, is through the seas. 85 per cent of our energy needs are imported through the sea. In the last financial year, 49.5 per cent of oil and 68 per cent of natural gas came from offshore fields. India is the fifth-largest producer of marine capture fisheries and the fourth-largest exporter of fish in the world. Therefore, our economy is inextricably linked with the oceans.

India's Vision for Indo-Pacific

India's vision for Indo-Pacific was laid out by the Prime Minister, in his speech at the Shangri La Dialogue in 2018.

> "India envisages a free, open, inclusive, peaceful and prosperous Indo-Pacific, built on a rules-based order and with sustainable and transparent infrastructure investments.
>
> It should have freedom of navigation and over-flight, unimpeded lawful commerce, mutual respect for sovereignty, peaceful resolution of disputes, and equality amongst nations."

ASEAN centrality and unity is an important element of the vision.

Subsequently in 2019, during the East Asia Summit in Thailand, the seven pillars of the Indo-Pacific Oceans Initiative (IPOI) were enunciated:

- Maritime security
- Maritime ecology
- Maritime resources
- Capacity building and resource sharing
- Disaster risk reduction and management
- Science, Technology & academic cooperation
- Trade, connectivity and maritime transport

Indo-Pacific Oceans Initiative (IPOI) aims to promote practical cooperation by drawing on existing regional architectures like the ASEAN-led East Asia Summit (EAS) framework, Indian Ocean Rim Association (IORA), BIMSTEC and the Pacific Island Forum (PIF). India's Act East Policy, Indian Ocean Naval Symposium (IONS), Forum for Indo-Pacific Islands (FIPIC), Indo-Pacific Oceans Initiative (IPOI) vision, establishment of IFC-IOR and deeper economic and defence cooperation have been shaping our engagement in the Indo-Pacific. The Quadrilateral Security Dialogue (QUAD) complements these initiatives.

Now I will talk about some unilateral initiatives of India that focus on the oceans.

- ***SAGAR (Security and Growth for All in the Region).*** The SAGAR vision builds upon the principles of cooperative measures for sustainable use of oceans. It has enabled enhanced MDA, assistance in EEZ surveillance, SAR, pollution control, and more for countries in the IOR.
- ***Act East.*** The Act East Policy focuses on the extended neighbourhood in the Indo-Pacific with ASEAN at its core. It promotes economic cooperation, and cultural ties and develops strategic relationships through bilateral, regional and multilateral engagements. Academic and Cultural linkages are further strengthened by MAUSAM.
- ***Blue Economy.*** To maintain its momentum of economic growth, India has identified the Blue Economy as one of the ten core dimensions of growth. It will contribute to food security, poverty alleviation, enhance trade & investment and improve maritime connectivity etc.
- ***Swachh Sagar, Surakshit Sagar.*** The focus of developing the Blue Economy is concomitant with sustainable and climate-resistant exploitation of resources. The Swachh Sagar Surakshit Sagar activity undertaken last year was focussed on cleaning up beaches and culminated on the International Coastal Clean Up Day (17 Sep 22). India is committed towards carbon neutrality as

exemplified during the PM's speech for the inauguration of Global Maritime India Summit 2023 and I quote "We are moving towards a future where the Blue Economy will be the medium to create a Green Planet".

IPRD 2023

While on one hand, there are multiple opportunities for our growth in the maritime domain, there also exist several challenges. Traditional security challenges, as well as non-traditional threats such as maritime terrorism, piracy, drug trafficking, illegal human migration and the rise of hybrid maritime threats, are impediments that we must overcome if we are to harness the potential of the 'Blue Economy'. Climate Change impact mitigation and adaptation is another important challenge, which calls for ongoing dialogues to be urgently translated into collaborative action. It is obvious that no one country, on its own, can address these challenges. Because more than 60 per cent of the earth's oceanic areas lie outside national jurisdictions, nations must come together to find solutions to these problems, most of which transcend national boundaries and maritime jurisdictions. Some of these include:

- ***Sea Bed Mining.*** Sea-bed mining for rare earth minerals has wide-ranging applications in high technology. This area, which is on the cusp of commercial exploitation, can rapidly accelerate into a race for competition, and possible contestation, in deep-sea mining. This could, in turn, increase the complexity of universally accepted legislation for regulating the common heritage of ocean resources leading to State-on-State conflicts.
- ***Undersea Cables.*** Similarly, undersea cables pose immense legal challenges even though they are indispensable for economic growth including that for smart ports.
- ***Cyberspace & MDA.*** Cyberspace will have an overarching influence on the development of ports and resilient maritime infrastructure by states and will remain an intensely contested domain due to the vested interests of non-state actors. These

issues highlight the absolute criticality of Maritime Domain Awareness (MDA) accompanied by space-based technologies.

Conclusion

In the context of ongoing and potential geo-politics and geo-economic contestations, I think, that the Indo-Pacific Regional Dialogue will play an important role in fostering regional ideation of sorts on issues about the maritime domain. Such dialogues help understand each other's perspectives.

I cannot emphasise enough the importance of 'dialogue' or 'Samvaad' in weaving the fabric of regional cooperation. It is the first step towards cooperation. And we in India, truly believe in the power of 'Samvaad'; perhaps we have inherited this quality from our ancient traditions where knowledge itself was imparted through the process of dialogue and discussion.

16

Transforming the Armed Forces Through Restructuring Technology and Atmanirbharta

Manohar Parrikar Institute of Defence Studies and Analyses
13th YB Chavan Memorial Lecture

23 Dec 2022

The subject of my talk today is a combination of four important and interrelated topics: Transformation, Technology, Restructuring and Atmanirbharta. Transformation and Change are intrinsic to the evolution of every organisation including the Armed Forces. Change, it is rightly said, is the only constant in life. The staccato periods of peace between wars and conflicts allow the Armed Forces to think about the challenges that lie ahead. No military in the world prepares for the last war. The outlook is always futuristic though one may always draw lessons from the past. As contemporary and ongoing conflicts have shown, multiple generations of warfare bleed into each other rather than fading away.

Change within the military is required since the environment keeps changing and transforming. The operational environment evolves with emerging threats, challenges, players, technologies, dimensions and methodologies, among others. In the domain of national security, due to the amorphous nature of the challenges, the Armed Forces have to deal with more intangibles than any other entity. The catch here is the accurate and correct visualisation of the future, difficult during the best of times. However, the ability to correctly predict trends will distinguish between success and failure and between victory and defeat. For military professionals, this ability will distinguish an amateur from a professional. Before talking about the future, let me elaborate on the nature of change itself. The change could be Adaptive, Transitional or Transformational.

Indian Armed Forces have been 'keeping pace with changing times' since Independence. They have been adaptive to the changing environment and based on 'experience', introduced changes.

A few examples are:

- Introduction of Mountain Divisions post 1962.
- Impetus to Mechanisation – learning from 1971 led to the creation of RAPID Divisions.
- Doctrinal changes like Cold Start or Proactive Strategy and interchanging roles between Pivot Formations and Strike Formations, post-Operation Parakram.
- Dynamic Response Strategy born out of the experience of Balakote air strikes and Operation Zafran.
- IBG models, currently under debate evolved as a result of Proactive Strategy and Dynamic Response Strategy.
- Large Force Engagement by the IAF or move towards net centricity by incorporation of Integrated Air Command and Control System (IACCS) nodes.
- Mission Based Deployment in the Indian Navy.

Adaptive change was the norm in the yesteryears since societal, technological and cultural factors changed gradually and one could envisage a sync between time and space. However, the current era of rapid and radical change necessitates the need for transformational change. No longer can we wait to adapt ourselves. Today, one needs to seize the day. Carpe Diem.

Military Transformation involves fundamental and comprehensive changes across the military domain, including doctrinal concepts; processes and procedures; force structures and organisations; capabilities and technology; and HRD or manpower issues.

Therefore, the Transformational Change that the Indian Armed Forces need to undertake will be in both the Cognitive and Physical Domains. The first to be transformed is the Cognitive Domain, which will determine the trajectory of the Transformation Process. Professional Military Education (PME) needs to be completely revamped with a focus on education rather than training. There is a subtle difference. We do understand that training is essential to prepare a soldier to act in a predetermined manner during the war, but it is the education that prepares him to predict and deal with emerging challenges and come up with innovative solutions. In the Cognitive Domain, all ranks, – from a soldier to a flag officer – will have to be conversant with the New Concepts of Warfighting, protocols and Tactics-Techniques & Procedures (TTPs).

In the Physical Domain, new equipment will require training, exploitation and maintenance protocols to change faster than ever before. Technology will have to be incorporated and discarded at a faster pace. Modern technology also dictates that the hierarchy should be flatter to enable faster decision-making in an environment of information overload. Winning the perception of people has a far greater effect than weapons. Strategic communication and exploitation of the information domain need to be seen as an element of national power. The ability to use technology to plan and integrate information campaigns will remain critical in fighting hybrid and contemporary warfare.

Military Reforms or Transformation cannot be done in isolation. It has to conform to the overall National Policy and needs. Military Concepts and Doctrines are a sub-set of Defence Strategy, which itself forms part of the overall National Security Architecture. The concept of National Security evolves continuously and incorporates many new domains into its folds. We are also attempting major reforms in defence that will have an impact on Military Strategy. Thus, our Doctrines and Concepts will need to undergo a fundamental change.

In the international domain, global geo-politics is in a state of flux. Today we witness a great churning of the established order. The recent and ongoing conflicts have major lessons for us in the political, diplomatic and military domains. Confining one to the military domain, one needs to introspect and inquire: given the dynamic and fast-changing situation, are the three services geared for the next big change? Are the existing organisational structures adequate to meet the next generational challenges? Do we need to restructure? Is the apex political leadership cognisant of the need for reforms and restructuring?

The simple answer to the last question is YES. The very purpose of creating the post of the CDS was to kick-start the process of defence reforms. The need for integration and creation of joint structures for joint planning, execution and joint conduct of military operations is only a subset of the larger defence reforms being attempted.

Modernisation and Atmanirbharta

Modernisation

The technological evolution of weapons and systems has altered the way we fight. Technology drives Modernisation which in turn is an important facet of Transformation. Modernisation aims primarily at bridging the gap between current capabilities and future requirements, ensuring the armed forces can effectively respond to emerging threats and scenarios. It encapsulates the integration of advanced technologies into military doctrine, strategy and tactics, facilitating a more dynamic, precise and efficient use of force. In essence, modernisation serves as a critical conduit through which militaries adapt to the rapid pace of technological change, enhancing their strategic posture and operational flexibility in the face of evolving geo-political landscapes. Modernisation is needed not only in equipment but also in processes, management and doctrinal concepts to cater for not only today's needs but also futuristic requirements.

Atmanirbharta

Atmanirbharta needs to be understood well beyond the domains of production, procurement and supplies. It means self-reliance and comes from the word "atman" which means from "within". It is also a state of mind related to self-confidence, self-relation and self-actualisation. It is not restricted to arms and ammunition or equipment alone but also relates to tactics, strategy and operational art. Defence Atmanirbharta is aimed at reducing foreign dependencies and replacing them with interdependencies, wherever required. Given the global situation, Atmanirbharta in Defence is the only way forward for India to ensure strategic autonomy as it marches to assume its rightful place in the world order.

Having missed the industrial revolution and the initial phases of the network-centric RMA, the Indian military needs to catch up with emerging technological changes. We need to address all three generations of RMA together. (We are not alone – all armies are in the middle of this huge uncertainty, flux and change). It will require a focused strategy, which includes:

- Need to Make in India, especially for the Military.
- Move from Atmanirbharta to Bharat Nirbharta (Make for the World).
- Indigenous solutions for the second and third generation of RMA (developing own software and own chips for ISR, decision-making, Battlefield domination and control etc).
- The New DAP, published in 2020, promotes Make in India. The five Positive Lists for import embargo on 509 items and setting up of new Defence Corridors in Tamil Nadu and Uttar Pradesh will provide a push to local industry.
- FDI has been enhanced from 49 per cent to 74 per cent. There is a push towards indigenisation with the policy of 2/3rd of defence budget procurements and 100 per cent procurements under Emergency Powers through the indigenous route.
- Corporatisation of the Ordnance Factories Board is aimed at improving their efficiency and increasing competition by providing a level playing field for the private players.
- Reforms have also been initiated to make DRDO more efficient. Eight Advance Technology Centres have been set up by DRDO for research on futuristic military applications such as AI, Quantum Technology, Smart Materials, etc).

The recent wave of reforms is, by far, the most elaborate one addressing the entire gamut such as increasing domestic defence production, access to critical technologies, encouraging investment to support indigenous industry and eventually aiming to tap the global market. The idea is to make India a Global Manufacturing Hub.

The efforts are already bearing fruits. On Sep 22, Hon'ble PM Shri Narendra Modi commissioned INS Vikrant with 76 per cent indigenous content at Kochi. With its induction, India has become only the sixth country to indigenously design and build an Aircraft Carrier. The recent induction of 'Prachand' LCH, developed by HAL, into the IAF at Jodhpur on 03 Oct 22, adds to the growing list of indigenously designed and developed weapon systems and equipment like LCA Tejas, K-9 Vajra, BrahMos Missile, ATAGs, ASTRA Missile, AKASH SAMs etc. These success stories are a testimony to our growing prowess in Indigenous design, development and manufacturing. These are significant milestones on the path to self-reliance.

However, maximising indigenous production without a well-supported R&D and export strategy may not reap the desired dividends. Indigenisation requires an integrated approach, collaboration and healthy competition between private players and DPSUs. We also need to gainfully engage with IITs, research institutes and academia to come up with potential solutions to some of our challenges. Also, Atmanirbhatra can fructify only when the Armed Forces assume the lead role in driving the technological developments for the Armed Forces. And that will come from the culture of original research and innovation in the education system as a whole.

Nature of Warfare

To initiate the Transformational Change, the Indian Armed Forces need to first decide, doctrinally and conceptually, how they intend to fight the next war or in fact, define what war is. Just as a pointer as to what is in store, especially for India, the recent conflicts demonstrate that conventional warfare is here to stay, but the outcomes on the battlefield will be dictated by technologies fielded by contestants.

I believe that geo-politics and geo-economics are changing the nature of war and technology is transforming its character.

As Rupert Smith said on the nature of war.

"There is no war – only contestations and conflicts."

It can be said that declared wars of the type we witnessed during WW I/ II, or in our context like the 1971 war, are a thing of the past. An all-out war is too costly, even if it does not escalate into the nuclear domain. War, in the conventional sense, has ceased to matter as an arbitrator of political affairs between states. Confrontation, conflict and combat undoubtedly exist all around the world, for which states still have Armed Forces, which they use as Symbols of Power. Nonetheless, War is cognitively known to most non-combatants; War is a battle in a field between men and machinery; or War is a massive deciding event in disputes in international affairs: such War no longer exists.

Look at the Ukrainian conflict. Although Russia described the war as a special operation, the actions on the ground resemble a conventional war as far as Ukraine is concerned. The West has spent close to 40 Billion US Dollars on Military Supplies alone to sustain the war. The US has otherwise granted aid amounting to nearly 100 Billion US Dollars on account of military and other aids. On the other hand, Russians have spent more than 82 Billion US Dollars in the war (according to Forbes). In terms of human losses, Russia has lost more than 10,000 troops whereas, as per US estimates, Ukraine has suffered more than 100,000 military casualties (both killed and wounded) and more than 40,000 civilian casualties.

The pervasiveness of information and the pace of technological change are transforming the character of war. Let us see how it has evolved thus far and what lies ahead. The simultaneity and synchronisation of the Air-Land battle or deep battles were possible due to enhanced surface and air mobility and the availability of long-range precision firing. This probably introduced the First Generation of Revolution in Military Affairs (RMA). The Second Generation of RMA occurred at the time of the conflict in Kosovo and later Desert Storm brought in the concept of

Battle Field Transparency and enhanced Situational Awareness. This concept based on net centricity, C4I2SR became an important part of the battlefield. Domination of the EW Spectrum was hence becoming important. The current phase or the Third Generation of RMA involves extreme automation such as Non-contact Warfare, Unmanned Platforms (or manned and unmanned teams) and Robotics.

The human element is slowly being removed not only from actual combat but also from the Decision-Making Loop. The latter is being aided by Artificial Intelligence (AI), Machine Learning (ML), Battle Damage Assessment (BDA), Internet of Things (IoT), etc. The next major change in warfare is that it has entered into the new domain of Cyber and Space. As the dependence of the World increases on Cyber and Space, these two domains are increasingly being used for either 'denial', 'disruption' or 'direct engagement'. In the domain of Cyber and Space, the concept of Sovereignty (which I will discuss a bit later) is yet to evolve, as these are currently being seen as Global Commons.

Reforms & Restructuring

The need for jointness is evident from the increasing list of common inventories that the three Services use such as MRSAMs, MANPADS (VSHRODs), ALH, MALE, HALE, UAVs, satellites, etc. The call for more integration is louder than ever before as is the aspect of optimum utilisation of such equipment.

Before talking about reforms or restructuring, I would like to talk about a few fundamentals i.e. Sovereignty and Essentials of Geography. These contribute to serve as building blocks on which the edifice of restructuring must be based.

Sovereignty

The concept of sovereignty on land is absolute. National boundaries are inviolable and our claims in disputed areas must be protected and promoted. Sovereignty in the air and maritime domain, both are dependent on land. Sovereignty in the air is also absolute. Infringement of air sovereignty is due to temporary Violations. In the maritime domain, the high seas are open for use by all. In the Territorial Waters, considered Sovereign (ie the water column, air space and sea bed), innocent passage by men of war is allowed under international laws, thus bringing forth its own set of challenges and opportunities. In cyber and space, sovereignty is shared by all and the concept of its violation is yet to evolve.

Geography

The strategic outlook of a nation is shaped by its Geography and historical experience. Those who do not understand geography are likely to be condemned by History. Geography impacts geo-politics, geo-economics and indeed strategic thinking of nations. India is a Continental power, connected by Geography to West- Asia, Central Asia and SE Asia; and a Maritime Power with a peninsular shape jutting into the IOR which has abundant Island territories. India cannot exploit the land bridge to connect with the rest of the world due to Pakistan and China. Disputed land borders impinge upon sovereignty and territorial integrity – a very sensitive issue. India needs the Seas/IOR to expand its economic influence and to connect with the rest of the world.

Continental and Maritime priorities need balancing as under:

- Continental for Security- Threat.
- Maritime for Exploitation – Opportunity.

The basic issue of geography points out that we need to have two Theatre Commands to look at the two threats/challenges we face in the continental domain and a Theatre Command to exploit opportunities in the IOR region (to secure our long-term interests). The limit of these Theatre Commands, wrt their role & responsibility is a matter of detail. This requires deliberations but the basic deduction arising out of the lessons of our geography and historical experience remains unchanged.

The process of restructuring into Theatre Commands involves both principles as well as processes. I think laying down principles is important. Some of the Principles that must pave the way for Theaterisation are:

- National Interests must override organisational/Service-specific interests.

- Creation of joint structures must be driven by operational considerations followed by logistic efficiency and HR issues in the last.
- Consensus amongst the three Services is the preferred approach. Changes must be driven by the Services.
- Integration should be time-bound – could be incremental or phased. Critical and challenging Sectors may be Theaterised first.
- Jointness is the key. The road to Theaterisation passes through jointness. The proposed integration must lead to operational and administrative efficiency.
- There should be NO ambiguity in the command-and-control structures for higher directions of war.
- Process of change must not affect operational preparedness.

I look at restructuring as a means to an end. Notwithstanding, we need to use resources prudently while enhancing the warfighting effectiveness of the Indian Armed Forces, to derive maximum advantage for National Security.

Conclusion

Humans have evolved because they have embraced change. Resistance to change is a universal phenomenon and it could be for many reasons; sometimes we are over-confident or at the other, we may fear change. But most of the time we simply ignore the glaring tell-tale signs till reality strikes hard. Increasing contestations in geo-politics, competition in geo-economics and the pervasiveness of technology are the hard realities that we need to be cognizant of. The change is inevitable but we must certainly choose the trajectory of the change to ensure the operational balance is retained at all times. Also, warfighting is a national effort and an integrated approach is the only way forward to develop structures, forces and equipment capable of dealing with such varied challenges. There is no alternative to indigenisation and self-reliance to ensure that the Strategic Autonomy is retained.

17

India's Quest for Strategic Autonomy: Opportunities and Challenges in the Emerging World Order

5th General KV Krishna Memorial Lecture

05 Oct 2023

India stands tall and independent in the world of power politics, guided by a simple yet powerful principle: strategic autonomy. This idea isn't new to us – it is woven into our history and identity. We, as a nation, have always aimed to make our own decisions, free from external pressures, whether choosing our friends or defining our adversaries. Today, as we face a world that's changing faster than ever – replete with new technologies, shifting power balances and complex threats – our commitment to strategic autonomy becomes even more crucial. It is about being strong enough to defend our interests and smart enough to build relationships that help us navigate these turbulent times. Strategic autonomy is not just trying to keep India safe; it also ensures that India stands firm in the international arena, defining its morality and way of existence.

I recall General Krishna Rao's famous book 'Prepare or Perish: A Study on National Security'. The book dealt with the hard choices a nation has to make to secure itself. Exercising autonomy in some manner is also about making choices in an environment of uncertainty and risk. It also assumes that the actor has the option of exercising that choice as a matter of first principles. Many nations do not possess this simple precondition of self-determination. We do and the choices we make will have a long-term impact on national security.

In any subject related to Diplomacy, National Security and international relations, there is an abstract world of theory and the real world of praxis. Today I'll talk about the evolution of the concept of strategic autonomy from what we practiced in the past which is non-alignment. Thereafter I will cover three important ingredients that help nations practice Strategic autonomy i.e. economic & military strength; partnerships & alliances; and self-reliance. Finally, I will talk about the exercise of strategic autonomy in the emerging world order.

Non-Alignment and Strategic Autonomy

Non-alignment has been an important cornerstone of Indian foreign policy ever since we became independent. India played a lead role not only in its conceptualisation but also in its practice. Looking back at non-alignment, one can say that it was a reaction to the bloc-based politics of the Cold War, where a newly independent India needed to retain adequate freedom from the two camps led by the USA and USSR, to formulate and chalk out its path on how to be a modern nation-state. Non-alignment passed away with the demise of the Soviet Union and the end of the Cold War. It gradually lost its relevance, at least in the context of Indian diplomacy. Strategic autonomy, in some way, is a more evolved and proactive form of Non-alignment. We all understand that absolute autonomy is not possible in a globalised and more importantly interconnected world of today. Hence, even in the exercise of autonomy, there has to be a 'Strategy' behind it. Strategic autonomy is not exercised in a vacuum. The choices we make in pursuit of national interests must be well considered and maintaining autonomy is part of that strategy.

Looking back at non-alignment, it thrived on not taking sides. Strategic autonomy is a far more active concept based on the idea of positive action and making choices – in the best interest of the nation. Non-alignment was non-assertive. Strategic autonomy is about 'power politics'. It is more pragmatic and visible.

Economic and Military Strength

Strategic autonomy denotes the ability to pursue national interests and adopt foreign policy without being excessively constrained. A state has to be powerful to exercise strategic autonomy. The shift in Indian diplomacy from being non-aligned to exercising strategic autonomy has been a gradual process. The world, including India, is at a pivotal moment in history. Extraordinary changes in the last two decades have fundamentally transformed India's economy and society. These changes have created the possibility of India exercising its economic heft to play a major role in the emerging geo-political milieu.

The economic heft of a nation is reflected in its military capability. A strong military is essential for the practice of strategic autonomy. Economic and Military strength create leverages for diplomacy to succeed. Indian leadership has demonstrated its ability to maintain strategic autonomy and make hard decisions in the nation's interest. It has been a slow but steady journey.

A successful series of nuclear tests in 1998 in the face of increasing pressure to accede to the CTBT was a test of Indian will to retain its ability to make strategic decisions in the national interest. India eventually became a victim of sanctions and the most severe technology denial regimes. It was a transitory phase in which India demonstrated its ability to make choices in the national interest and be prepared for the consequences that follow. 25 years later, in taking a neutral and nuanced stand on the Russia-Ukraine conflict, India demonstrated its steadfast adherence to its principle of strategic autonomy. Despite the looming threats of sanctions based on CAATSA, India went ahead with the purchase of S-400 missiles as well as the import of cheaper Russian crude. This time the strategic autonomy was being exercised by a different India – a stronger and more resilient India. There was also a greater understanding and acceptability of India's viewpoint within the broader community of nations. It was India's purchase of cheap Russian crude oil and subsequent sale of refined oil products to the Europeans which prevented a spike in oil prices across the globe when a so-called price cap had been imposed on Russian oil.

Partnerships and Alliances

I believe that India has transited ahead from the Non-Alignment of yesteryears to multi-alignment. This was reflected in the recent statement of the EAM at the UNGA. He said, "India has evolved from the era of Non-Alignment to the era of Vishwa Mitra – a friend to the world." Multi-alignment adds a different dimension within the diplomatic world in terms of making choices.

Exercising Choices or strategic decision-making is more complex in today's environment. Countries are part of alliances and partnerships in bilateral, multilateral, plurilateral & mini-lateral forums. India is not only part of UN G-20 but also SCO, BRICS, I2U2 and QUAD at the same time. This strategy requires balancing relationships with multiple nations, organisations and international groups and at the same time, walking a tightrope on contentious issues between mutual partners of India. Being part of alliances or partnerships helps maintain autonomy in strategic decision making but at times some decisions have to be made, keeping the larger interest of the Group or the World. India while advocating the philosophy of 'Vasudhaiva Kutumbakam' on issues like Global Warming and Climate Change will decide on the larger interest of the world. The theme of the G-20 Summit during India's presidency was 'One Earth, One Family, One Future' which is a pointer towards such trends.

In the last century, during the outbreak of World War I & World War II, most alliances had a predominantly military dispensation. The structure of SEATO, CENTO, NATO and the Warsaw Pact was a natural outcome of the concept of The Axis and Allied powers in World War II. Some global leaders also advocate being 'allied' yet remaining non-aligned. However, in today's world, the global balance of power is impacted by economic interests, technological sovereignty challenges and management of Global interests. In India's famous epic of Mahabharata, Lord Krishna shifted the balance of power in favour of Pandavas by joining them but without his military might. His military power went to the Kauravas. Sage advice and righteousness were key in shifting the balance of power. It is even relevant today. We as a nation righteously utilised the G20 platform to leverage our soft power to play a dominating role.

Atmanirbharta and Self-Reliance

Atmanirbharta, Self-Reliance and Make in India or Make for the World are some initiatives, especially in the field of defence manufacturing, which have a major role to play in maintaining India's strategic autonomy. Unfortunately, we have not understood the concept of 'Atmanirbharta' in its entirety, which has to be taken out of the narrow arena of defence manufacturing. In Self-reliance, the focus is on the self. So is it in Atmanirbharta where Atman – the Inner self-assumes importance? Knowing oneself or 'Atman' is important. It will lead to Self-realisation – Self-actualisation. Self-reliance and Self-confidence are important offshoots of it. Indigenisation or Indian ideas must guide our strategic thought and culture. Our history should be the source of our motivation. A truly Atmanirbhar Bharat – a nation which has its strategic thinking and does not rely for its major defence needs on foreign OEMs will help us in the maintenance of Strategic autonomy. One has to be clear that self-reliance or Atmanirbharta is in no way a clarion call for autarky. It is only a self-reliant India, a powerful India, which can truly be a Vishwa Mitra.

Emerging World Order

The global geo-political environment is currently in a state of flux. The world is transiting between two orders. The old-world order is withering away. The new one is yet to evolve. The shapes and contours of the new order are difficult to predict accurately. The current flux is also being labelled as World Disorder. The geo-economic situation, like geo-politics, is also in a state of flux. Repetitive financial crises, disruption of global supply chains, food and fertiliser shortages due to the Russia-Ukraine conflict, and renewed calls for delinking and de-risking economies from

China due to tensions in the South China Sea and Taiwan are manifestations of this flux. Technological disruptions are even more stark. Increased focus on climate tech such as hydrogen fuel cell batteries, EVs, shortage of specialised chips, Rare earths, and advancement in AI, ML, and Big Data – all will have a profound impact on society, businesses and trades.

Challenges and Opportunities

It is said that opportunities come at a time of disruption. What we are witnessing is a great disruption in geo-political, geo-economic and geo-technological domains. The decisions or choices India makes today will decide where it will stand in the comity of nations in the future. Threats and Challenges for the country are well known. It is easy to make choices when dealing with Threats and Challenges as they are identifiable, quantifiable and predictable. Making the right choices when opportunities present themselves will be the acme of our diplomacy. Towards this, our strategic policies must be rooted within the framework of promoting the larger righteous national interest without being constrained or under external pressure.

In its strategic calculus, India will have to take into account the emergence of China as a major power. China's assertiveness is more evident with its rise. India has a major dispute on its Northern border with China. India will have to play its strategic autonomy cards very carefully. If I were to summarise India's Journey from Non-Alignment to exercising Strategic Autonomy, it must be based on what I call as 'Principles of Three S'.

- ***Securing India.*** The first principle is 'Securing India from external as well as internal threats' – the foremost priority.
- ***Self-Reliance.*** The second principle of 'Augmenting the Self-Reliant potential of India' so that we reduce our dependencies and increase our capabilities to support and shape the environment.
- ***Shaping the Environment.*** Following the first two principles will

lead to the third principle of 'Shaping the environment favourably for India'. This will ensure a larger participative role in global affairs.

Conclusion

As EAM Dr S Jaishankar states in his book "The India Way", it is "time for India to engage America, manage China, cultivate Europe, reassure Russia, bring Japan into play, draw neighbours in, extend the neighbourhood and expand traditional constituencies of support." – all the while continuing to grow economically, reforming and strengthening the democratic system. Today's talk is, to a large extent, captured in the statement of our EAM.

18

Artificial Intelligence (AI) Transforming Warfare

CAPSTAR

Military Institute of Technology

Keynote Address
Gen Anil Chauhan, PVSM, UYSM, AVSM, SM, VSM

17 Jan 2024

> *"Artificial Intelligence is a tribute to human intellectual power."*
>
> —Narendra Modi, Hon'ble PM of India

Today, as we stand at the precipice of a new era, it is impossible to ignore the pervasive impact of AI. Simply put, artificial intelligence is the culmination of human ingenuity, a fusion of science and technology that aims to replicate human intelligence in machines.

The technology that began with humble aspirations has now evolved into a force that permeates every facet of our lives. From the days of Alan Turing, a British computer pioneer, to the present, AI has come a long way.

Today, AI is not just a buzzword, it is a tangible force driving innovation across industries. As we marvel at the strides humans have made in this field, it is important to acknowledge the pioneers who laid the groundwork for this transformative journey.

Falguni Desai, an author, speaker and corporate strategist, defined AI as,

> "Artificial Intelligence is about replacing human decision-making with more sophisticated technologies."

The roots of AI can be traced back to ancient history when philosophers and thinkers contemplated the nature of thought and reasoning.

However, the formal birth of AI can be attributed to the mid-20th century, marked by the groundbreaking work of pioneers such as Alan Turing. Turing, in his seminal paper on "Computing Machinery and Intelligence" in 1950, laid the conceptual foundation for AI by posing the question: "Can machines think?" This question sparked the imagination of scientists and set the stage for the birth of a new era.

The journey of AI which started as a science fiction, has seen a complete reorientation. It has now been woven into the fabric of our daily life – education, healthcare, finance, commerce, transportation – the list is endless. But let me focus today on its effect on military operations and its impact on warfare.

Changing Dimensions of Warfare

Before I go into the specifics of how AI will impact future warfare, let me briefly mention how warfare itself is transforming. The traditional dimensions of war have witnessed an expansion and now straddle a Continuum where Crisis, Confrontation, Conflict and War exist together in varying gradations. The traditional domains of warfare have witnessed a convergence with new domains of Cyber and Space with an underpinning of Information in all domains. New technologies like AI, Robotics, Quantum and IoT are coming together and making the battle space more automated and autonomous.

As per my visualisation, we are witnessing what I call 'Convergence Warfare'. Here, the conventional notions of physical might are transcending to an arena where mastery over skills like Data Analytics and Artificial Intelligence is fast becoming the linchpin of military success on the battlefield.

Role of Artificial Intelligence in Warfare

From the early days of cryptography to the current era of autonomous systems, AI has emerged as a strategic asset. It aids in analysing vast amounts of data, providing real-time insights and predicting potential threats. Today, it is a force that is increasingly being used for enhancing ISR, logistics, maintenance, battlefield support and various decision-making functions critical for the armed forces. Concerning the specifics, today's warrior faces two main challenges: Decision-making in the presence of a humungous amount of data, and operating in the complex and congested battlefield. These two major challenges guide humans to look for intelligent assistive solutions.

During the development of machines based on the so-called 'Human Intelligence loop', militaries are also looking for specific solutions. These solutions are being obtained concurrently with the progress of development happening in three waves:

- The first wave concerns the use of AI in Machines that assist in data comparison and selection of a course of action based on pre-defined algorithms. Such machines have provided solutions which aid in ISR, cyber security, simulation and predictive assessments.
- The next wave is the development of machines with cognitive capabilities wherein Robotics and Machine Learning along with AI are being used for the development of autonomous and unmanned battle support solutions. These solutions with kinetic capabilities are the ones which force nations to undertake ethics-related deliberations.
- The third wave, still in the experimentation phase, is the development of machines that use AI for Contextual Adaptation. This is where new products and advancements like Generative AI are being achieved. It is believed that Machines may develop human power of reasoning, prediction and intuitive action in the long term. It will provide nations and militaries solutions in areas where human employment faces severe restrictions.

The transformative capabilities of AI are building an environment where military forces are undertaking synergetic application of human expertise and machine intelligence. Increased employment of unmanned systems in recent conflicts and the development of concepts like Manned-Unmanned Teaming (MUM-T) are certain early trends. Such a transformative environment is forcing nations to build specific AI adoption strategies and reorient their investments. Nations are also finding common forums to discuss associated challenges and build an agreeable framework to ensure the responsible use of AI in the military. These unprecedented deliberations are the indicators of the potential of AI and the likely shape it is going to take in the future.

Developments in India: Artificial Intelligence

In the Indian context, we as a nation have adopted a mission-mode approach towards Artificial Intelligence. At the national level, NITI Aayog adopted a three-pronged approach – undertaking exploratory proof-of-concept AI projects, crafting a national strategy for building a vibrant AI ecosystem and collaborating with various experts and stakeholders. A National Strategy for Artificial Intelligence (NSAI) by NITI Aayog was formulated in 2018. Based on the national-level strategy, multiple initiatives have been taken by various ministries. Specific committees in these ministries have been addressing AI issues related to policy enabling, skill building, capability enhancements and safety (legal and ethical). Platforms like India-AI and IDeX, are being utilised to grow capabilities and establish a customised growth trajectory for the country.

Under the Ministry of Defence (MoD), a multi-agency Defence AI Council (DAIC) has been established and an associated Joint working mechanism between MoD, HQ IDS and Service HQs has been put into action. Centres of Excellence (CsOE) have been set up both at national and military levels to work in key areas. A total of 67 projects are being steered by the Services and are at various stages of development.

We as a nation have also adopted a global collaborative approach to build capabilities. The recent announcement of the joint India-US initiative on Critical and Emerging Technologies (CET) is one such action which will provide the necessary boost in our technology-building capabilities.

The domain-agnostic nature of AI necessitates the building of a global regulatory framework to ensure the safe and trustworthy use of AI while we harness its potential. India as the chair of GPAI has articulated a similar thought while believing in the responsible use of AI. I am sure that these outlines will assist India and the Indian Armed Forces to build the desired canvas in the field of AI.

Conclusion

AI offers us not just a technological edge but a strategic advantage in addressing various challenges. The journey ahead demands our collective commitment. It would assist us to shape a future where technology serves as a force multiplier not only for security but also for peace, stability and the protection of our values. It will assist India to leapfrog technologically and quicken the pace of our quest to be a developed nation.

19

Emerging Role of Young Generation

144th NDA Passing Out Parade

Gen Anil Chauhan, PVSM, UYSM, AVSM, SM, VSM

30 May 2023

Lines from Rudyard Kipling's immortal poem 'IF', still kept in the cabin of each cadet, encapsulate the training and mindset of this institution. I quote a few lines,

> If you can dream and not make your dreams your master.
>
> If you can meet with Triumph and Disaster and treat them just the same.
>
> If you can walk with Kings and not lose the common touch.
>
> Yours is the Earth and everything that's in it and what is more you will be a Man my son.

and may I add 'If you can serve the country by placing your service before self, you will be a true soldier'.

I also noticed a few women cadets as part of the parade. I congratulate them for breaking through into the male bastion. I am glad that you have chosen to shoulder equal responsibility as your male counterparts to defend the national interest.

Before you take the decisive final step or Antim Pag into your respective service academies and follow in the footsteps of your illustrious predecessors and heroes, I would like to remind you of the lines of the NDA prayer – 'Choose the harder right instead of the easier wrong'. A harder right may lead to temporary setbacks but remember, a bend in the road is not the end of the road. Treat success and failure with equanimity.

Once in service, you should follow the principle of humility and simplicity as a true virtue. Remember 'Simplicity is the ultimate sophistication and Humility is the solid foundation of all virtues'.

You must also imbibe an Indian outlook and draw inspiration from indigenous thoughts to motivate the troops under your command. If the bravery enshrined in the 'Charge of the Light Brigade' by Lord Alfred Tennyson inspires you, our men are equally likely to be inspired by 'Khoob ladi mardana woh to Jhansi wali Rani thi' of Subhadra Kumari Chauhan. You need to create a judicious mix of the two.

We are living in a time where the global security situation is not at its best and the international geo-political order is in a state of flux. The war in Europe, the continued deployment of PLA in strength along our Northern borders, and political and economic turmoil in our immediate neighbourhood – all present different forms of challenges to the Indian military. The armed forces are committed to maintaining the legitimacy of our claims on the Northern borders and play a constructive role in maintaining peace and stability in our immediate and extended neighbourhood.

We are also witnessing a new revolution in military affairs, mostly driven by technology. The process of this 'change', driven by advanced and disruptive technology, is only going to accelerate your service time. You will need to be well-informed and adaptive to meet the demands of transformation and change to be 'future-ready' for combat at all times.

The Armed Forces of India are also on the path of major reforms. Jointness, Integration and creation of Theatrised Commands is on the anvil. The spirit of jointness imbibed by you in NDA will act as a catalyst to speed up these reforms. I want you to further this spirit as you grow in service.

Index